KT-525-249

KNIT & CROCHET 50 ACCESSORIES

COLLINS & BROWN

Contents

Hats 68

Socks 128

Bags 186

Mittens

Stay warm and make an impression with a pair of mittens. If you are a beginner try the Marshmallow Muff or the Striped Mittens to get you going. Looking to work on advanced skills? Hone your colourwork skills with the Fair Isle Warmers or work an advanced stitch pattern with the Textured Gloves. Remember to do a tension (gauge) swatch before starting or it might be a tight squeeze to fit your hand in!

DESIGNED BY

Spot-On Mittens

Made with an array of colourful polka dots, these toasty hand-warmers really hit the spot. The yarn carried across the back of the work adds a double thickness.

YARN

Jamieson & Smith 2-ply Jumper Weight (100% wool), approx. 25g (1oz)/115m (126yd) per ball

- Five balls of Cream 1A **(MC)**
- Five balls of Deep Blue FC37 **(A)**
- Five balls of Pink FC6 **(B)**
- Five balls of Pale Blue FC15 **(C)**
- Five balls of Deep Pink 72 **(D)**

NEEDLES

Pair of 3.25mm (US 3) knitting needles
Pair of 2.75mm (US 2) knitting needles

EXTRAS

Two stitch markers
Tapestry needle

TENSION (GAUGE)

28 sts and 36 rows = 10cm (4in) square measured over St st using 3.25mm (US 3) needles.

TO FIT

One size

SKILL LEVEL

Intermediate

SPECIAL ABBREVIATIONS

See page 255 for information on three-needle cast (bind) off.

PATTERN

Row 1: K24 in MC, PM, m1 in MC, k2 in MC, m1 in MC, PM, knit to end in MC.

Row 2: P1 in MC, [p2 in MC, 2 in A, 2 in MC] four times, k2 in MC, 2 in A, 1 in MC, SM, p1 in MC, 2 in A, 1 in MC, SM, p1 in MC, 2 in A, 2 in MC, [p2 in MC, 2 in A, 2 in MC] three times, p1 in MC.

Row 3: K1 in MC, [k1 in MC, 4 in A, 1 in MC] three times, k1 in MC, 4 in A, SM, m1 in MC, k4 in A, m1 in MC, SM, k4 in A, 1 in MC, [p1 in MC, 4 in A, 1 in MC] four times, k1 in MC.

Row 4: P1 in MC, [p1 in MC, 4 in A, 1 in MC] four times, p1 in MC, 4 in A, SM, p1 in MC, 4 in A, 1 in MC, SM, p4 in A, 1 in MC, [p1 in MC, 4 in A, 1 in MC] three times, k1 in MC.

MITTENS (MAKE 2)

Using 2.75mm (US 2) needles and MC, cast on 57 sts.
Work in k1, p1 rib for 6cm (2½ in), dec 1 st at end of last row. (56 sts)
Change to 3.25mm (US 3) needles and St st.

THUMB GUSSET

Starting at Row 1, work from chart as follows:

Row 1 (RS): Patt 24, PM, m1, k2, m1, PM, patt to end.

Row 2: Patt 30, SM, patt 4, SM, patt to end.

Row 3: Patt 24, SM, m1, patt 4, m1, SM, patt to end.

Row 4: Patt 30, SM, patt 6, SM, patt to end.

Row 5: Patt 24, SM, m1, patt 6, m1, SM, patt to end.

Row 6: Patt 30, SM, patt 8, SM, patt to end.

Row 7: Patt 24, SM, m1, patt to next marker, m1, SM, patt to end.

Row 8: Patt 30, SM, patt to next marker, SM, patt to end.

Rep last two rows six times more until Row 20 of chart has been worked and there are 22 sts between the two markers.

THUMB

Row 1: In MC, k46, turn, cast on 2 sts. Starting at Row 2 (WS), work from chart as follows:

Row 2: Patt 24 (including two newly cast-on sts), turn, cast on 2 sts (in D).

Rows 3–19: Starting with a knit row, work 17 rows on these 26 sts until Row 19 has been completed.

SHAPE TOP

Row 20 (WS): [P2tog in MC, p1 in MC, p2tog in D, p1 in MC] four times, p2tog in MC. (17 sts)

Cut off all contrast yarns and cont in MC only.

Row 21: K1, [k2tog] to end of row. (9 sts)
Cut off yarn, thread through rem sts, draw up and fasten off.
Sew seam.

MAIN SECTION (BOTH MITTENS)

Row 1: With RS facing, rejoin yarn (MC), pick up and knit 2 sts at base of thumb and knit to end of row. (56 sts)

Rows 2–20: Starting with Row 2 (WS), work 19 rows of chart until Row 20 has been completed.

SHAPE TOP

Rows 21–34: Follow chart from Row 21 to Row 34.

Row 35: K1 in MC, k2tog tbl in MC, patt 23, k2tog in C, k2tog tbl in C, patt 23, k2tog in MC, k1 in MC.

Row 36: Work Row 16 of chart (all in MC).

Row 37: K1 in MC, k2tog tbl in MC, patt 21, k2tog in D, k2tog tbl in D, patt 21, k2tog in MC, k1 in MC.

Row 38: Work Row 18 of chart.

Row 39: K1 in MC, k2tog tbl in MC, patt 19, k2tog in D, k2tog tbl in D, patt 19, k2tog in MC, k1 in MC.

Row 40: Work Row 20 of chart.

Row 41 (all in MC): K1, k2tog tbl, k17, k2tog, k2tog tbl, k17, k2tog, k1.

Row 42: Work Row 2 of chart.

Row 43: K1 in MC, k2tog tbl, patt 15, k2tog in A, k2tog tbl in A, patt 15, k2tog in MC, k1 in MC.

Row 44: Patt 16, p2tog tbl in A, p2tog in A, slip this st back onto LH needle. Weave two sets of sts together using Kitchener st (see page 256), changing colour according to sts being grafted.

Alternatively, turn mitten inside out and
use three-needle cast (bind) off.

FINISHING

Sew in loose ends and block lightly. Sew
side seam.

ON THE SPOT

Why not use a darker colour for
the main colour of the mitten and
add white or cream spots to
complement it?

Key

☐ MC ☐ C
■ A   ■ D
■ B

DESIGNED BY

Gosia Dzik-Holden

Textured Gloves

These easy-going gloves take you from day to night without missing a beat.

YARN
Debbie Bliss Alpaca Silk DK (80% alpaca, 20% silk), approx. 50g (1¾oz)/105m (115yd) per ball
Four balls of Yellow 15

NEEDLES
Set of five 2.00mm (US 0) double-pointed needles (dpns)

EXTRAS
Cable needle
Two spare needles
Tapestry needle

TENSION (GAUGE)
14 sts and 16 rows = 5cm (2in) square measured over St st using 2.00mm (US 0) needles.

TO FIT
One size

SKILL LEVEL
Advanced

SPECIAL ABBREVIATIONS
See page 254 for information on MB and C4R.

SCHIAPARELLI STITCH

Worked in 4 rounds over an even number of sts.

Crossed st (Cr st): Insert RH needle through front loop of first st on LH needle from right to left and then knit second st through front loop from this position, without taking either stitch off the needle, then knit the first st still on the needle tbl.

Round 1: [Cr st] to end.
Rounds 2 and 4: Knit.
Round 3: K1, [Cr st] to last st, k1.

RIGHT GLOVE

ARM

Using Continental method, cast 64 sts onto one dpn. Divide sts evenly across four dpns (16 sts per needle). Join for working in the round, being careful not to twist sts, and PM after first st to denote beg of round.

Round 1: Knit.
Round 2: [P1, k1, p1, MB] to end.
Rounds 3–4: [P1, k1] to end.
Rounds 5–6: Knit.
Round 7 (cable round): C4R, [Cr st] to end.
Round 8: Knit.
Round 9: K5, [Cr st] to last st, k1.
Round 10: Knit.
Round 11: As Round 7.
Round 12: As Round 8.
Round 13: As Round 9.
Round 14: K to last st, slip last st to RH needle.

Round 15 (cable and dec round): Place 2 sts on cn and hold at back of work, slip slipped st from RH needle to LH needle; k2tog, k1, k1 from cn, slip second st knitwise from cn to RH needle, k1, psso, k1, [Cr st] to last st, k1.
Round 16: Knit.
Round 17: K4, [Cr st] to end.
Round 18: Knit.
Round 19 (cable round): C4R, k1, [Cr st] to last st, k1.
Round 20: Knit.
Round 21: K4, [Cr st] to end.
Round 22: K to last st, slip last st to RH needle.
Round 23 (cable and dec round): Place 2 sts on cn and hold at back of work, transfer slipped st from RH needle to LH needle, k2tog, k1, k1 from cn, slip second st knitwise from cn to RH needle, k1, psso, [Cr st] to end.
Rounds 24–87: Rep Rounds 8–23 four times more. (44 sts)
Work 11 rounds even.
Rounds 99–104: As Rounds 8–13.
Round 105: Knit.
Round 106: C4R, [Cr st] to end.
Round 107: Knit.
Round 108: K5, [Cr st] to last st, k1.
Round 109: Knit.
Round 110: C4R, [Cr st] to end. Work should measure about 25.5cm (10in).
Round 111: K4, m1, k to last st, m1. (46 sts)

SHAPE THUMB

Round 1: K4, [Cr st] ten times. Rearrange sts so that next 6 sts are on sep needle for thumb section (TS), knit these 6 sts, knit to end of round.
Round 2: Knit.
Round 3 (cable round): C4R, k1, [Cr st] nine times, k to end.
Round 4 (inc round): K4, m1, k to end, m1. (48 sts)
Round 5 (thumb inc round): K5, [Cr st] ten times; TS: k1, m1, k4, m1, k1; k to end. (50 sts)
Round 6: Knit.
Round 7 (cable round): C4R, [Cr st] ten times, k to end.
Round 8 (inc round): K4, m1, k to end, m1. (52 sts)
Round 9: K4, [Cr st] eleven times, k to end.
Round 10 (thumb inc round): K26; TS: k1, m1, k6, m1, k1; k to end. (54 sts)
Round 11 (cable round): C4R, k1, [Cr st] ten times, k to end.
Round 12 (inc round): K4, m1, k to end, m1. (56 sts)
Round 13: K5, [Cr st] eleven times, k to end.
Round 14: Knit.
Round 15 (thumb inc and cable round): C4R, [Cr st] eleven times, k1; TS: k1, m1, k8, m1, k1; k to end. (58 sts)
Round 16 (inc round): K4, m1, k to end, m1. (60 sts)

Round 17: K4, [Cr st] twelve times, k to end.

Round 18: Knit.

Round 19 (cable round): C4R, k1, [Cr st] eleven times, k to end.

THUMB

Round 1: K28; TS: k6, take new needle and knit rem 6 sts of TS, take another new needle and cast on 6 sts using loop method; close work and cont in St st until approx. 0.75cm (³/₈in) shorter than desired length.

Next round: [K2tog, k1] six times. (12 sts)

Next round: Knit.

Next round: [K2tog] to end. Cut off yarn, thread through 6 rem sts and pull tight to close gap.

PALM OF HAND

Pick up 9 sts along line of thumb cast-on and knit to end of round. (57 sts)

Round 2: K4, [Cr st] twelve times, k to end.

Round 3: K to last st, slip last st to RH needle.

Round 4 (cable and dec round): Place 2 sts on cn and hold at back of work, transfer slipped st from RH needle to LH needle, k2tog, k1, k1 from cn, slip second st knitwise from cn to RH needle, k1, psso, [Cr st] eleven times, k to end of round. (55 sts)

Round 5: Knit.

Round 6: K5, [Cr st] eleven times, k to end.

Round 7: K to last st, slip last st to RH needle.

Round 8 (cable and dec round): Place 2 sts on cn and hold at back of work, transfer slipped st from RH needle to LH needle, k2tog, k1, k1 from cn, slip second st knitwise from cn to RH needle, k1, psso, k1, [Cr st] ten times, k to end. (53 sts)

Round 9: Knit.

Round 10: K4, [Cr st] ten times, k to end.

Round 11: K to last st, slip last st to RH needle.

Round 12 (cable and dec round): Place 2 sts on cn and hold at back of work, transfer slipped st from RH needle to LH needle, k2tog, k1, k1 from cn, slip second st knitwise from cn to RH needle, k1, psso, [Cr st] nine times, k to end. (51 sts)

Round 13: Knit.

Round 14: K5, [Cr st] nine times, k to end.

Round 15: K to last st, slip last st to RH needle.

Round 16 (cable and dec round): Place 2 sts on cn and hold at back of work, transfer slipped st from RH needle to LH needle, k2tog, k1, k1 from cn, slip second st knitwise from cn to RH needle, k1, psso, k1, [Cr st] eight times, k to end. (49 sts)

Round 17: Knit.

Round 18: K4, [Cr st] eight times, k to end.

Round 19: K to last st, slip last st to RH needle.

Round 20 (cable and dec round): Place 2 sts on cn and hold at back of work, transfer slipped st from RH needle to LH needle, k2tog, k1, k1 from cn, slip second st knitwise from cn to RH needle, k1, psso, [Cr st] seven times, k to end. (47 sts)

Round 21: Knit.

FINGERS

On finishing last round, k first 2 sts of cable and then divide the total 47 sts over two needles, with 2 sts of cable on each needle.

LITTLE FINGER

Round 1: K6; using loop method, cast 3 sts onto new needle; transfer last 6 sts of the last round to spare needle. Slip 1 st from each needle to one with newly cast-on sts – 5 sts on each needle. (15 sts)
Work these 15 sts in round until approx. 0.75cm (³/₈in) shorter than desired length is reached.

Next round: [K2tog, k1] to end. (10 sts)

Next round: Knit.

Next round: [K2tog] to end. Cut off yarn, thread through rem sts and pull tight to close gap.

THIRD FINGER

Pick up 3 sts cast on for little finger, k5 along upper side of hand, cast on 4 sts, k5 along inner side of hand. (17 sts) Work as for little finger.

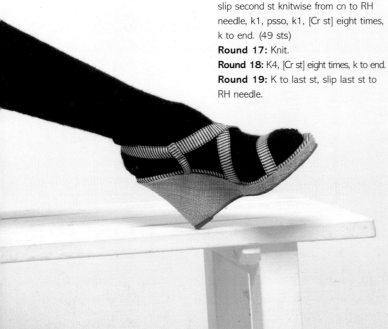

SECOND FINGER

Pick up 4 sts cast on for third finger, k5 along upper side of hand, cast on 4 sts, k5 along inner side of hand. (18 sts)
Work as for little finger.

FIRST FINGER

Pick up 4 sts cast on for second finger, k15 along upper and inner side of hand. (19 sts)
Work as for little finger.

LEFT GLOVE

Work as for Right Glove to Round 111.

SHAPE THUMB

Round 1: K20, place next 6 sts on sep needle, knit these 6 sts and then [Cr st] ten times.
Round 2: Knit.
Round 3 (cable round): C4R, k23, [Cr st] nine times, k1.
Round 4 (inc round): K4, m1, k to end, m1. (48 sts)
Round 5 (thumb inc round): K21; TS: k1, m1, k4, m1, k1; [Cr st] ten times, k1. (50 sts)
Round 6: Knit.
Round 7 (cable round): C4R, k26, [Cr st] ten times.
Round 8 (inc round): K4, m1, k to end, m1. (52 sts)
Round 9: K30, [Cr st] eleven times.
Round 10 (thumb inc round): K22; TS: k1, m1, k6, m1, k1; k to end. (54 sts)

Round 11 (cable round): C4R, k29, [Cr st] ten times, k1.
Round 12 (inc round): K4, m1, k to end, m1. (56 sts)
Round 13: K33, [Cr st] eleven times, k1.
Round 14: Knit.
Round 15 (thumb inc and cable round): C4R, k19; TS: k1, m1, k8, m1, k1; k1, [Cr st] eleven times. (58 sts)
Round 16 (inc round): K4, m1, k to end, m1. (60 sts)
Round 17: K36, [Cr st] twelve times.
Round 18: Knit.
Round 19 (cable round): C4R, k33, [Cr st] eleven times, k1.

THUMB

Round 1: K24; TS: k6, take new needle and knit rem 6 sts of TS, then take another new needle and cast on 6 sts using loop method; close work and cont in St st until approx. 0.75cm (³/₈in) shorter than desired length.
Next round: [K2tog, k1] six times. (12 sts)
Next round: Knit.
Next round: [K2tog] to end. Cut off yarn, thread through rem 6 sts and pull tight to close gap.

PALM OF HAND

Pick up 9 sts along line of thumb cast on and knit to end of round. (57 sts)
Round 2: K33, [Cr st] to end.
Round 3: K to last st, slip last st to RH needle.

Round 4 (cable and dec round): Place 2 sts on cn and hold at back of work, transfer slipped st from RH needle to LH needle, k2tog, k1, k1 from cn, slip second st knitwise from cn to RH needle, k1, psso, k29, [Cr st] to last st, k1. (55 sts)
Round 5: Knit.
Round 6: K32, [Cr st] to end.
Round 7: K to last st, slip last st to RH needle.
Round 8 (cable and dec round): Place 2 sts on cn and hold at back of work, transfer slipped st from RH needle to LH needle, k2tog, k1, k1 from cn, slip second st knitwise from cn to RH needle, k1, psso, k28, [Cr st] to last st, k1. (53 sts)
Round 9: Knit.
Round 10: K31, [Cr st] to end.
Round 11: K to last st, slip last st to RH needle.
Round 12 (cable and dec round): Place 2 sts on cn and hold at back of work, transfer slipped st from RH needle to LH needle, k2tog, k1, k1 from cn, slip second st knitwise from cn to RH needle, k1, psso, k27, [Cr st] to last st, k1. (51 sts)
Round 13: Knit.
Round 14: K30, [Cr st] to end.
Round 15: K to last st, slip last st to RH needle.

Round 16 (cable and dec round):
Place 2 sts on cn and hold at back of
work, transfer slipped st from RH needle
to LH needle, k2tog, k1, k1 from cn,
slip second st knitwise from cn to RH
needle, k1, psso, k26, [Cr st] to last st,
k1. (49 sts)
Round 17: Knit.
Round 18: K29, [Cr st] to end.
Round 19: K to last st, slip last st to
RH needle.
Round 20 (cable and dec round):
Place 2 sts on cn and hold at back of
work, transfer slipped st from RH needle
to LH needle, k2tog, k1, k1 from cn,
slip second st knitwise from cn to RH
needle, k1, psso, k25, [Cr st] to last st,
k1. (47 sts)
Round 21: Knit.

FINGERS
On finishing last round, k first 2 sts of
cable and then divide the total 47 sts
over two needles, with 2 sts of cable on
each needle.

LITTLE FINGER
Round 1: K6; using loop method, cast
3 sts onto new needle; transfer 6 sts
of the last round to spare needle. Slip
1 st from each needle to one with
newly cast-on sts – 5 sts on each
needle. (15 sts)
Work these 15 sts in round until
approx. 0.75cm (⅜in) shorter than
desired length is reached.

Next round: [K2tog, k1] to end. (10 sts)
Next round: Knit.
Next round: [K2tog] to end. Cut off
yarn, thread through rem sts and pull
tight to close gap.

THIRD FINGER
Pick up 3 sts cast on for little finger, k5
along upper side of hand, cast on 4 sts,
k5 along inner side of hand. (17 sts)
Work as for little finger.

SECOND FINGER
Pick up 4 sts cast on for third finger, k5
along upper side of hand, cast on 4 sts,
k5 along inner side of hand. (18 sts)
Work as for little finger.

FIRST FINGER
Pick up 4 sts cast on for second finger,
k15 along upper and inner side of hand.
(19 sts)
Work as for little finger.

FINISHING
Turn the gloves inside out and sew in all
loose ends.

ROUND UP

After working first round of palm,
transfer 1 st to each side of new
cast-on sts from neighbouring
needles, to avoid irregular sts in
these areas.

DESIGNED BY

Rose-Button Gauntlets

These charming hand-warmers are simple to make in double (single) crochet. The pretty lace panel at the wrist is decorated with a row of small crocheted rose buttons.

YARN

Lana Grossa Royal Tweed (100% wool), approx.
50g (1¾oz)/100m (109yd) per ball
   One ball of Pink 26 **(MC)**
   One ball of Tangerine 21 **(A)**
Rowan Cashcotton 4-ply (35% cotton, 25% polyamide,
18% angora, 13% viscose, 9% cashmere), approx.
50g (1¾oz)/180m (197yd) per ball
   One ball of Pretty 902 **(B)**

HOOK

One 5.50mm (I/9) crochet hook

EXTRAS

Tapestry needle

TENSION (GAUGE)

11 sts and 13 rows = 10cm (4in) square measured over
double (single) crochet using 5.50mm (I/9) hook.

TO FIT

One size

SKILL LEVEL

Beginner

RIGHT GAUNTLET

Foundation chain: Using A, begin at the cuff end and make 24 ch plus 1 ch as tch, turn.

Row 1 (WS): 1 dc (sc) in each ch across, 1 ch, turn. (24 sts)

Row 2 (RS): 1 dc (sc) in each dc (sc) across, 1 ch, turn.

Rep last row three times more, ending with ss (sl st) in last dc (sc) to fasten off A, turn.

Row 6 (RS): Join in MC to ss (sl st) (counts as first st), 1 ch, 1 dc (sc) in each dc (sc) across, 1 ch, turn.

Row 7 (WS): 1 dc (sc) in each dc (sc) across, ending 1 dc (sc) in ss (sl st), 1 ch, turn.

Row 8 (RS): 1 dc (sc) in each dc (sc) across, 1 ch, turn.

Rep last row five times more, join with ss (sl st) in first dc (sc) (does not count as st) to form ring and cont to work in rounds. (24 sts)

Round 1: Miss ss (sl st), 1 dc (sc) in each dc (sc) around, ss (sl st) in first dc (sc).

Rounds 2–3: As Round 1.

ADD THUMB

Round 4: 2 dc (sc) in next dc (sc), 1 dc (sc) in each dc (sc) around, ss (sl st) in first dc (sc). (25 sts)

Rounds 5–7: As Round 4. (28 sts)

SHAPE THUMB

Round 8: 2 dc (sc) in next dc (sc), 1 dc (sc) in each of next 3 dc (sc), miss next 20 dc (sc), 1 dc (sc) in each of next 4 dc (sc) – this shapes the thumb. (9 sts)

Cont to work on the thumb only.

Round 9: 1 dc (sc) in each of next 9 dc (sc).

Round 10: As Round 9.

Fasten off.

HAND

Join in A to rem 20 dc (sc) to st at inside edge of thumb, then cont to work in rounds to complete the hand.

Round 1: 2 dc (sc) in next dc (sc), 1 dc (sc) in each of next 20 dc (sc). (21 sts)

Round 2: 1 dc (sc) in each of next 21 dc (sc).

Rounds 3–6: As Round 2. Fasten off.

LACY EDGING

With top of glove uppermost and thumb facing right, join yarn B with ss (sl st) to dc (sc) beneath thumb at opening on right front edge.

Row 1: 1 ch, 1 dc (sc) in each of next 13 dc (sc) down to cuff, 1 ch, turn. (13 sts)

Row 2 (WS): Miss first dc (sc), 1 dc (sc) in each of next dc (sc), ending 1 dc (sc) in 1 ch, 1 ch, turn.

Row 3: Miss first dc (sc), *miss 1 dc (sc), 5 tr (dc) in next dc (sc), miss 1 dc (sc), 1 dc (sc) in next dc (sc); rep from * to end.

Fasten off.

LEFT GAUNTLET

Work as for Right Gauntlet to Lacy Edging.

LACY EDGING

With top of glove uppermost and thumb facing left, join on B with ss (sl st) to dc (sc) beneath thumb at opening on left front edge. Work as for Right Gauntlet.

ROSE BUTTON

Foundation row: Using MC, make 4 ch.

Round 1: 10 dc (sc) in fourth ch from hook, working over loose end.

Fasten off, leaving a tail of yarn for sewing it to the gauntlet.

Make two alike in MC, and four in C.

FINISHING

Use the buttons to join the opening in the gauntlet. Sew three buttons in order: one MC at cuff, then two C, evenly spaced, to front of lacy edging. When buttons are in position, turn glove inside out and secure yarn at back. Sew in all loose ends.

DESIGNED BY

Striped Mittens

These simple stripy mittens are the same front and back. A nubbly, tweedy yarn adds textural and visual interest to a traditional design.

YARN

Debbie Bliss Donegal Aran Tweed (100% wool), approx. 50g (1¾oz)/88m (96yd) per ball

    Two balls of Black 01 **(MC)**
    One ball of Natural 04 **(A)**

NEEDLES

Pair of 4.50mm (US 7) knitting needles
Pair of 4.00mm (US 6) knitting needles

EXTRAS

Two stitch markers
Two small stitch holders
Tapestry needle

TENSION

18 sts and 26 rows = 10cm (4in) square measured over St st using 4.50mm (US 7) needles.

TO FIT

One size

SKILL LEVEL

Beginner

SPECIAL ABBREVIATIONS

See page 254 for information on m1l and m1r.

MITTENS (MAKE 2)

Using 4.50mm (US 7) needles and MC, cast on 41 sts.

Row 1 (RS): [K1, p1] to last st, k1.
Row 2: [P1, k1] to last st, p1.
These 2 rows form rib. Work as set for 7.5cm (3in), ending with a WS row.
Row 3: Knit.
Row 4: Purl.
These 2 rows form St st.

THUMB GUSSET

*Change to A.
Row 1 (RS): K20, PM, m1, k1, m1, PM (3 sts between markers), k20. (43 sts)
Note: On further rows, slip markers as you reach them.
Row 2: Purl.
Change to MC.
Row 3: Knit.
Row 4: Purl.**
Work in stripe pattern as set from * to **, alt 2 rows in each colour. Do not cut off yarn between stripes.

Cont inc the gusset as on Row 1 until 13 sts between markers. (53 sts)
Work 3 rows straight in St st, ending with a WS row in MC.
Next row (RS): With A, knit to first marker; slip 13 gusset sts onto a holder to be worked later, dropping markers; kfb, work to end of row. (41 sts)
Cont to work in St st stripes until hand measures 6.5cm (2½ in) from top of gusset, ending with a WS row in MC.

SHAPE TOP

Cut off A and cont with MC in St st to top of mitten as follows:
Row 1 (RS): K1, skpo, k35, k2tog, k1. (39 sts)
Row 2 and all WS rows: Purl.
Row 3: K1, skpo, k33, k2tog, k1. (37 sts)
Row 5: K1, skpo, k31, k2tog, k1. (35 sts)
Change to 4.00mm (US 6) needles.
Row 7: K1, skpo, k12, k2tog, k1, skpo, k12, k2tog, k1. (31 sts)
Row 9: K1, skpo, k10, k2tog, k1, skpo, k10, k2tog, k1. (27 sts)
Row 11: K1, skpo, k8, k2tog, k1, skpo, k8, k2tog, k1. (23 sts)
Row 13: K1, skpo, k6, k2tog, k1, skpo, k6, k2tog, k1. (19 sts)
Row 14: Cast (bind) off purlwise.

MAKE THUMB

Slip 13 sts from holder to 4.00mm (US 6) needle. Join in MC and cont to end of thumb:
Next row (RS): Kfb, knit to last st, kfb. (15 sts)
Work in 7 rows St st.

SHAPE TIP

Row 1 (RS): [K1, k2tog] to end. (10 sts)
Row 2: Purl.
Row 3: [K2tog] to end. (5 sts)
Cut off yarn, leaving end long enough to sew thumb seam.
Thread end through rem sts and pull tight to close gap.

FINISHING

Sew thumb seam. With RS facing, sew side and top seams, taking care to match stripes. Sew in all loose ends.

ZEBRA CROSSING

For neat edges and smooth seams, insert the needle as if to work the next stitch after completing the first stitch in every row. Before completing the stitch, give the working yarn a gentle pull to tighten up the edge, then continue across row.

DESIGNED BY

Sue Bradley

Ribbon Wrist-Warmers

Satin ribbons add a pretty detail to these quick-knit fingerless gloves. For some extra sparkle or colour, stitch a few beads to the back of the hand.

YARN

Rowan Soft Tweed (56% wool, 20% viscose, 14% polyamide, 10% silk), approx. 50g (1¾oz)/80m (87yd) per ball

   Two balls of Antique 002

NEEDLES

Pair of 5.00mm (US 8) knitting needles
Pair of 7.00mm (US 10½) knitting needles

EXTRAS

Stitch holder
3m (3½yd) of 10–15mm (⅜–⅝in) wide satin ribbon
Sewing needle and thread
Tapestry needle

TENSION (GAUGE)

13 sts and 18 rows = 10cm (4in) square measured over St st using 7.00mm (US 10½) needles.

TO FIT

One size

SKILL LEVEL

Beginner

LOVE THIS? Try the Ribbon Socks by Ellen Mallett on page 150.

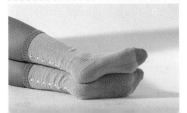

WRIST-WARMERS (MAKE 2)

Using 5.00mm (US 8) needles, cast on 28 sts.

Rows 1–10: [K1, p1] to end.

Change to 7.00mm (US 10½) needles and knit 2 rows.

Row 13: Knit.

Row 14: Purl.

These 2 rows form St st. Rep once more.

Row 17: Knit, wrapping yarn around needle (yrn) twice on every stitch of row.

Row 18: Purl, dropping yrn.

Work 4 rows in St st.

MAKE LACE HOLES

Row 23: [K2, yo, k2tog] to end.

Row 24: Purl.

Row 25: [K1, yo, k2tog, k1] to end.

Row 26: Purl.

Work 2 rows in St st.

Rows 29–30: As Rows 17–18.

THUMB GUSSET (LEFT MITTEN)

Row 1: K11, kfb, k2, kfb, k13. (30 sts)

Row 2: Purl.

Row 3: K11, kfb, k4, kfb, k13. (32 sts)

Row 4: Purl.

Row 5: K11, kfb, k6, kfb, k13. (34 sts)

Row 6: Purl.

Note: For right mitten, work in reverse by beginning each RS row with k13 and ending with k11.

THUMB (LEFT MITTEN)

Row 1: K21, turn and leave rem 13 sts on stitch holder.

(For right mitten k22, turn and leave rem 12 sts on stitch holder.)

Row 2: Cast on 2, p10, turn and leave rem sts on stitch holder, cast on 2 sts. (12 sts)

Work 4 rows in St st.

Knit 2 rows.

Cast (bind) off.

With RS facing, knit across all sts on stitch holder. (26 sts)

Work 3 rows in St st.

Next row: Knit, wrapping yarn around needle (yrn) twice on every stitch of row.

Next row: Purl, dropping yrn.

Work 2 rows in St st.

Knit 2 rows.

Cast (bind) off.

FINISHING

Sew in all loose ends and lightly press pieces under a damp cloth. With right sides together, sew up edges of mitten and thumb seams.

RIBBON DECORATION

Cut six 30cm (12in) lengths of ribbon to thread through the dropped stitch rows, and two 45cm (18in) lengths of ribbon to thread through the lace holes. Turn mitten inside out and neatly hand-stitch one end of the ribbon to the side seam. Now thread the ribbon into a large tapestry needle, or safety pin, and use this to thread the ribbon in and out of the dropped stitches/lace holes. Stitch the other end of the ribbon carefully to the side seam.

NO STRINGS ATTACHED

If you want to lengthen the cuff, simply work a longer rib. To add a hint of whimsy, embellish with a patterned ribbon.

DESIGNED BY

Fair Isle Warmers

Suited to the knitter with some experience, this adorable design made with an eye-catching palette is sure to capture your heart. Why not make them as a gift for that special loved-one?

YARN

Debbie Bliss Cashmerino Chunky (55% merino wool, 33% microfibre, 12% cashmere), approx. 50g (1¾oz)/65m (71m) per ball

- One ball of Fuschia 05 **(A)**
- One ball of Magenta 07 **(B)**
- One ball of Lime 12 **(C)**
- One ball of Taupe 14 **(D)**
- Two balls of Chocolate 15 **(E)**
- One ball of Slate 20 **(F)**
- One ball of Burnt Orange 16 **(G)**

NEEDLES

Set of five 4.50mm (US 7) double-pointed needles (dpns)

EXTRAS

Cable needle (or spare dpn)
Stitch holder
Tapestry needle

TENSION (GAUGE)

18 sts and 23 rows = 10cm (4in) square measured over St st using 4.50mm (US 7) needles.

TO FIT

One size

SKILL LEVEL

Intermediate

SPECIAL ABBREVIATIONS

See page 254 for information on C2F.

NOTE

These gloves are worked inside out, with the Fair Isle section mostly in reverse stocking (stockinette) stitch; this helps to prevent the colour stranding from pulling the fabric in and making the gloves too small.

As the dimensions are given in cm/in rather than specific rounds, each new sequence begins with Round 1.

Remember to twist the yarn in as the pattern moves: this will make for smaller floats, which is important when trying to fit the gloves correctly.

GLOVES (MAKE 2)
BODY

Using E and Continental method, cast on 36 sts. Divide sts evenly across four dpns and slip last st onto cn.

Round 1: K1, k1 from cn to secure bridge, [k1, p1] to end.

Work k1, p1 rib until cuff measures 6cm (2¼ in) – approx. 15 rounds.

At the beg of next round, change stitch to moss (seed) stitch as follows:

Round 1: *P1, k1; rep from * to end.

Round 2: *K1, p1; rep from * to end.

Rep these 2 rows for 5 rounds, ending on a Round 1 rep.

Next round: Change colour and purl to end.

Work in purl from this point until end of Fair Isle pattern (with the exception of 2 rows in the middle).

The pattern is knitted in rounds from the inside as reverse stocking (stockinette) stitch.

Refer to chart for Fair Isle pattern and colour change directions. Cont with patt, including 2 rounds of continuous knit (stocking (stockinette) stitch) towards the top, until the glove body measures 19.5cm (7¾ in) – approx. 50 rounds.

THUMB GAP

At the beg of the next round, work the sts straight, so working in rows rather than rounds. This results in a fork at the beginning/end of the rows.

Cont with the Fair Isle pattern and into moss (seed) st on the hand throughout these rows; when knitting moss (seed) st, work the same sequence as before. After 3 rounds of moss (seed) st, when thumb gap measures 4.5cm (1¾ in), resume working in rounds: work the row until the last st, then use C2F to bridge the gap as before.

UPPER HAND

Cont working in moss (seed) st for upper hand until it measures 3cm (1¼ in) from the top of the thumb gap; 27cm (11 in) in total length.

FINGERS

Note: Fingers are worked starting with the little finger. For all fingers you must knit half the sts before you work the sequence, so the placement will be at the opposite end to the thumb gap.

LITTLE FINGER

Next round: Work 18 sts (half total round), work 4 sts, place foll 28 sts on stitch holder, leaving final 4 sts to work for little finger. Divide these 8 sts between three dpns.

Next round: Work moss (seed) st to last st, C2F to bridge gap (using the 2 sts on either side of the hand gap).

Next 2 rounds: Work moss (seed) st.

Next 2 rounds: [K1, p1] to end.

Cast (bind) off 8 sts.

In order for the placement of the other fingers to be slightly higher than that of the little finger, 1 round must be completed before starting on next finger. Rejoin the yarn at the bridged finger gap to pull the gap together. Work 1 round in moss (seed) st.

THIRD FINGER

Next round: Work 4 sts, place foll 20 sts on stitch holder, leaving final 4 sts to work for third finger. Divide these 8 sts between three dpns.

Next round: Work moss (seed) st to last st, C2F to bridge gap.

Next 3 rounds: Work moss (seed) st.

Next 2 rounds: [K1, p1] to end.

Cast (bind) off 8 sts.

SECOND FINGER

Rejoin yarn at the bridged finger gap, work 5 sts, place foll 10 sts on stitch holder, leaving 5 sts to work for second finger. Divide these 10 sts between three dpns.

Next round: Work moss (seed) st to last st, C2F to bridge gap.

Next 3 rounds: Work moss (seed) st.

Next 2 rounds: [K1, p1] to end.

Cast (bind) off 10 sts.

FIRST FINGER

Rejoin yarn at the bridged finger gap and make 2 sts by picking up the bar at the middle finger bridge, leaving 12 sts to divide between four needles.

Round 1: Work moss (seed) st to last st, C2F to bridge gap.

Next 4 rounds: Work moss (seed) st.

Next 2 rounds: [K1, p1] to end.

Cast (bind) off 12 sts.

FINISHING

Sew in all loose ends and reinforce finger joins.

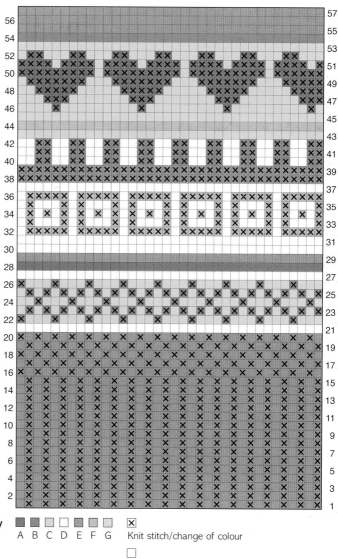

Key

A	B	C	D	E	F	G	☒ Knit stitch/change of colour

☐ Reverse St st

DESIGNED BY

Marshmallow Muff

This gorgeous, super-soft hand-warmer in luxurious mohair, which can be worn on its own or with a detachable cord that goes around the neck or through a jacket, is an ideal project for a quick fix of knitting.

YARN

Rowan Romance (36% acrylic, 27% nylon, 26% mohair, 8% polyester, 3% wool), approx. 50g (1¾oz)/55m (60yd) per ball

Two balls of Glitter 090 **(A)**
Two balls of Sparkle 095 **(B)**

NEEDLES

Pair of 7.00mm (US 10½) knitting needles
Two 4.00mm (US 6) double-pointed needles (dpns)

EXTRAS

Tapestry needle
Piece of stiff paper/cardboard for pompoms
Two small metal D-rings
Two 38mm (1½ in) press studs (snap fasteners)

TENSION (GAUGE)

12½ sts and 16 rows = 10cm (4in) square measured over St st using 7.00mm (US 10½) needles and yarn doubled.

TO FIT

One size

SKILL LEVEL

Beginner

INVISIBLE SHOULDER SEAM

Insert the needle behind the first stitch, under the cast-on row on the outer tube from right to left, and bring the needle through to the front of the work. Now insert the needle from right to left behind the corresponding stitch on the inner tube and then bring it through to the front of the work. Alternating from outer to inner, work around the tube.

MUFF

Using 7.00mm (US 10½) needles and A doubled, cast on 46 sts.

Row 1: Knit.

Row 2: Purl.

These 2 rows form St st.

Using B doubled:

Row 3: Knit.

Row 4: Purl.

Pick up A and cont to work straight in St st, alt A and B every other row, for 104 rows. Cast (bind) off, leaving a long tail for sewing up the muff.

POMPOMS (MAKE 4)

Cut two identical discs of cardboard measuring 4cm (1½ in) in diameter. Cut a hole, 2cm (¾ in) in diameter, in the centre of both discs. Cut off approx. 270cm (3yd) of A.

Place the discs together. Pass the yarn through the centre of the hole and wrap around the outside of the discs, making sure the discs are uniformly covered. Now cut the yarn at the edge of the discs by positioning the scissors in between the two pieces of cardboard. Take a piece of yarn 40cm (15in) long and, leaving one short tail and one long, wrap it very tightly in between the two discs, around the cut pieces, and tie a knot. Remove the cardboard discs and fluff out the pompom – you may need to trim it to make an even sphere. Trim off the short tail.

STRAP

Using 4.00mm (US 6) dpns and B, cast on 3 sts and knit 1 row. Without turning work, slide the sts to the other end of the needle, pull yarn tight across the back and knit the next row.

Continue to knit and slide in this way until the strap measures 114cm (45in), then cast (bind) off. You may need to give the cord a tug as you go to pull it into a tube. Do not sew in ends.

FINISHING

With RS of muff facing, sew up the long sides using mattress stitch (see page 255); do not fasten off. Fold the muff in half, and you will now have a double-thickness tube.

With RS facing, sew up the end as you would an invisible shoulder seam (see above). Sew in all loose ends.

Rearrange tube so that the seam is centrally placed inside the muff.

Attach D-rings to either end of the muff.

Attach press studs (snap fasteners) to either end of the strap.

Tie the two pompoms to each side of the strap and thread strap through D-rings.

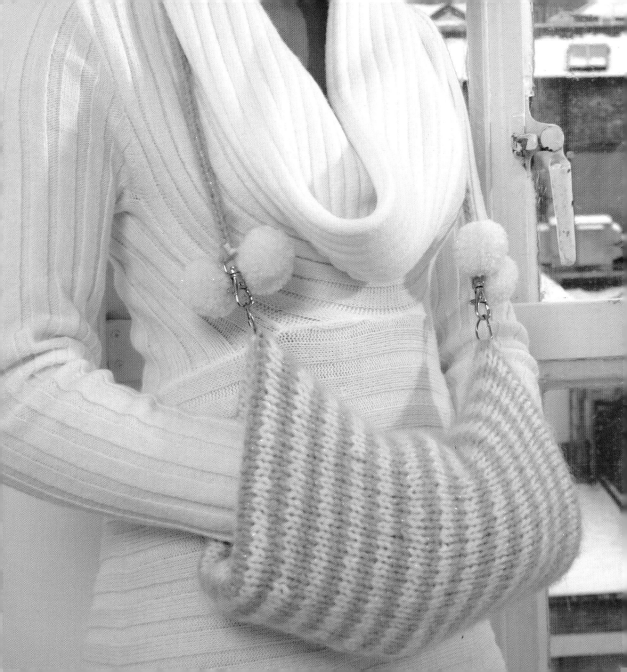

DESIGNED BY

Flip-Top Mitts

The multicoloured yarn creates an amazing kaleidoscope effect on these cosy crocheted mittens. Adjust the size by adding more rows before shaping the top.

YARN

Rowan Tapestry (70% wool, 30% soybean fibre), approx. 50g (1¾oz)/
120m (131yd) per ball
  Two balls of Rainbow 171

NEEDLES

One 4.00mm (G/6) crochet hook

TENSION (GAUGE)

18 sts and 9 rows = 4in (10cm) square measured over treble (double) crochet using 4.00mm (F/5) hook.

TO FIT

One size

SKILL LEVEL

Intermediate

SPECIAL ABBREVIATIONS

See page 255 for information on trtog.

MITTENS (MAKE 2)

Make 41 ch.

Row 1: 1 dc (sc) into second ch from hook, 1 dc (sc) into each ch to end.

Row 2: 1 ch, 4 dc (sc), miss 4 dc (sc), *9 tr (dc) into next dc (sc), miss 3 dc (sc), 1 dc (sc) into next dc (sc), miss 3 dc (sc); rep from *, ending 1 dc (sc) in last dc (sc), turn.

Row 3: 3 ch, miss first dc (sc), tr4tog (dc4tog) over next 4 tr (dc), *4 ch, 1 dc (sc) into next tr (dc) (the centre of the 9 tr (dc)), 3 ch, tr9tog (dc9tog) over [next 4 tr (dc), 1 dc (sc), 4 tr (dc)]; rep from *, ending tr5tog (dc5tog) over [last 4 tr (dc) and 1 ch], turn.

Row 4: 3 ch, 4 tr (dc) in top of tr5tog (dc5tog), *1 dc (sc) into next dc (sc), miss 3 ch, 9 tr (dc) into top of tr9tog (dc9tog); rep from *, ending 5 tr (dc) into top of tr4tog (dc4tog), turn.

Row 5: 3 ch, miss first tr (dc), *tr9tog (dc9tog) over [next 4 tr (dc), 1dc (sc), 4 tr (dc)], 3 ch, 1 dc (sc) into next tr (dc) (the centre of 9 tr (dc)), 3 ch; rep from *, ending 1 dc (sc) into top of tch, turn.

Row 6: 1 ch, miss first dc (sc), *miss 3 ch, 9 tr (dc) into top of tr9tog (dc9tog), miss 3 ch, 1 dc (sc) into next dc (sc), rep from *, working last dc (sc) into top of 3 ch, turn.

Rows 3–6 form pattern. Rep Rows 3–6 once more, then Rows 3–4 once again. Fasten off.

TOP

Make 35 ch plus 2 tch.

Row 1: 1 tr (dc) into third ch from hook, 1 tr (dc) into each ch to end, turn (35 sts).

Row 2: 2 ch, 1 tr (dc) into each tr (dc) of previous row, turn. Rep this row 2 five times.

SHAPE TOP

Next row: 2 ch, tr2tog (dc2tog) as foll: (*yoh and insert into next st, yoh and draw through, yoh and under first 2 loops on hook; rep from * once more, yoh and under all 3 loops on hook), 13 tr (dc), tr2tog (dc2tog), 1 tr (dc), tr2tog (dc2tog), 12 tr (dc), tr2tog (dc2tog), 1 tr (dc), turn (31 sts).

Next row: 2 ch, tr2tog (dc2tog), 11 tr (dc), tr2tog (dc2tog), 1 tr (dc), tr2tog (dc2tog), 10 tr (dc), tr2tog (dc2tog), 1 tr, turn (27 sts).

Next row: 2 ch, tr2tog (dc2tog), 9 tr (dc), tr2tog (dc2tog), 1 tr (dc), tr2tog (dc2tog), 8 tr (dc), tr2tog (dc2tog), 1 tr (dc), turn (23 sts).

Next row: 2 ch, tr2tog (dc2tog), 7 tr (dc), tr2tog (dc2tog), 1 tr (dc), tr2tog (dc2tog), 6 tr (dc), tr2tog (dc2tog), 1 tr (dc), turn (19 sts).

Fasten off.

THUMB

Make 4 ch and ss (sl st) into first ch to form a ring.

Round 1: 2 ch, 9 tr (dc) into ring, ss (sl st) into top of ch at beg of round.

Rounds 2–5: 2 ch, 1 tr (dc) into each tr (dc) of prev round, join with ss (sl st) into top of ch at beg of round.

Round 6: 1 ch, 1 dc (sc) into each of next 3 tr (dc), 2 tr (dc) into next tr (dc), 1 tr (dc), 2 tr (dc) into next tr (dc), 1 dc (sc) into next each of 3 tr (dc), ss (sl st) into top of 1 ch at beg of round (11 sts).

Round 7: 1 ch, 1 dc (sc) into each of next 3 sts, 2 htr (hdc) into next st, 2 tr (dc) into next st, 1 tr (dc), 2 tr (dc) into next st, 2 htr (hdc) into next st, 1 dc (sc) into each of next 3 sts, ss (sl st) into top of 1 ch at beg of round (15 sts).

Round 8: 1 ch, 1 dc (sc) into each of next 5 sts, 2 htr (hdc) into next st, 2 tr (dc) into next st, 1 tr (dc), 2 tr (dc) into next st, 2 htr (hdc) into next st, 1 dc (sc) into each of next 5 sts, ss (sl st) into top of 1 ch at beg of round (19 sts).

Round 9: 1 ch, 1 dc (sc) into each of next 7 sts, 2 htr (hdc) into next st, 2 tr (dc) into next st, 1 tr (dc), 2 tr (dc) into next st, 2 htr (hdc) into next st, 1 dc (sc) into each of next 7 sts, ss (sl st) into top of 1 ch at beg of round (23 sts).

Cut off yarn.

FINISHING

Sew in all loose ends and block fabric. Place a marker at centre point of both mitten top and base. Pin Top to the inside of Mitten base along Row 10. Using backstitch, sew into position up to the centre point marker. Fold mitten top in half and stitch top and sides together.

Fold mitten base in half, stitch up to Row 4, then stitch together Rows 10 upwards. Pin Thumb to gap and stitch in place. When stitching top flap in position, remember that for the left, stitch to the right side of the base; for the right, stitch to the left of the base. This will ensure that both mittens flip in the same direction.

DESIGNED BY

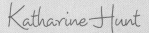

Cable Mittens

These warm and cosy mittens are knitted in a smart Donegal tweed and have an easy-to-work bobbly cable pattern running up the back of the hand.

YARN

Debbie Bliss Donegal Aran Tweed (100% wool), approx.
50g (1¾oz)/88m (96yd) per ball
  Two balls of Purple 07

NEEDLES

Pair of 4.50mm (US 7) knitting needles
Pair of 4.00mm (US 6) knitting needles

EXTRAS

Cable needle
Two stitch markers
Two small stitch holders
Tapestry needle

TENSION (GAUGE)

18 sts and 24 rows = 10cm (4in) square measured over St st using 4.50mm (US 7) needles.

TO FIT

One size

SKILL LEVEL

Intermediate

SPECIAL ABBREVIATIONS

See page 254 for information on FC, BC and MK.

BOBBLY CABLE PATTERN

Panel worked over 15 sts.

Rows 1, 3, 5, 7 (WS): K5, p5, k5.
Row 2: P5, k2, MK, k2, p5.
Row 4: P5, MK, k3, MK, k5.
Row 6: P5, k2, MK, k2, p5.
Row 8: P4, BC, p1, FC, p4.
Row 9: K4, p2, k1, p1, k1, p2, k4.
Row 10: P3, BC, k1, p1, k1, FC, p3.
Row 11: K3, p3, k1, p1, k1, p3, k3.
Row 12: P2, BC, [p1, k1] twice, p1, FC, p2.
Row 13: K2, p2, [k1, p1] three times, k1, p2, k2.
Row 14: P2, k3, [p1, k1] twice, p1, k3, p2.
Rows 15, 17, 19: As Rows 13, 11 and 9.
Row 16: P2, FC, [p1, k1] twice, p1, BC, p2.
Row 18: P3, FC, k1, p1, k1, BC, p3.
Row 20: P4, FC, p1, BC, p4.
Rep Rows 1–20 twice more, then Rows 1–7 once. This completes Bobbly Cable Pattern panel.

RIGHT MITTEN

Using 4.50mm (US 7) needles, cast on 41 sts.
Work 3 rows in k1, p1 rib, ending with a RS row.
Row 4 (WS): Rib 23 sts, work Row 1 of Bobbly Cable Pattern (CP) over next 15 sts, p1, k1, p1.
Cont working in rib and CP as set, until end of the first cable rep – cuff measures approx. 9cm (3½ in), ending with a RS row. Rib cuff is now complete.
Cont in CP, working background in Rev St st throughout as foll:
Next row (WS): K23, CP15, k3.
Work 2 more rows as set.

THUMB GUSSET

Row 1 (RS): P3, CP15, p2, PM, m1, p1, m1, PM (3 sts between markers), p20. (43 sts)
Note: On subsequent rows, slip each marker.
Row 2: K25, CP15, k3.
Row 3: P3, CP15, purl to end.
Row 4: As Row 2.
Keeping CP as set, cont inc gusset at markers as on Row 1 on every 4th row until there are 13 sts between markers. (53 sts)
Work 3 rows even, ending with a WS row.
Next row (RS): Work to first marker, slip 13 gusset sts onto stitch holder to be worked later, dropping markers. Kfb and work to end of row. (41 sts)
Cont to work in patt as set until hand measures 6.5cm (2½ in) from top of gusset, ending with Row 1 of CP.

SHAPE TOP

Row 1 (RS): P1, p2tog, CP15, p20, p2tog tbl, p1. (39 sts)
Row 2 and all WS rows: Work even.
Row 3: P1, p2tog, CP14, p19, p2tog tbl, p1. (37 sts)
Row 5: P1, p2tog, CP13, p2tog tbl, p1, p2tog, p13, p2tog tbl, p1. (33 sts)

Change to 4.00mm (US 6) needles.
Row 7: P1, p2tog, p11, p2tog tbl, p1, p2tog, p11, p2tog tbl, p1. (29 sts)
Row 9: P1, p2tog, p9, p2tog tbl, p1, p2tog, p9, p2tog tbl, p1. (25 sts)
Row 11: P1, p2tog, p7, p2tog tbl, p1, p2tog, p7, p2tog tbl, p1. (21 sts)
Row 12: Cast (bind) off knitwise.

THUMB

Slip 13 sts from holder to 4.00mm (US 6) needle and rejoin yarn.
Row 1 (RS): Pfb, p to last st, pfb. (15 sts)
Work in Rev St st for 7 rows.

SHAPE TOP

Row 1: [P1, p2tog] across row. (10 sts)
Row 2: Knit.
Row 3: P2tog across row. (5 sts)
Cut off yarn, leaving end long enough to sew thumb seam.
Thread yarn through remaining sts, draw up and fasten securely.

LEFT MITTEN

Using 4.50mm (US 7) needles, cast on 41 sts.
Work 3 rows in k1, p1 rib, ending with a RS row.
Row 4 (WS): Rib 3 sts, work first row of CP over next 15 sts, rib 23.
Cont working in rib and CP as set, until end of the first cable rep and end of ribbed cuff as on Right Mitten, ending with a RS row.

Next row (WS): K3, CP15, k23.
Work 2 more rows as set.

THUMB GUSSET
Row 1 (RS): P20, PM, m1, p1, m1,
PM, p2, CP15, p3 (3 sts between
markers). (43 sts)
Row 2: K3, CP15, knit to end.
Row 3: P25, CP15, p3.
Row 4: As Row 2.
Keeping CP as set, cont inc gusset at
markers as on Row 1 on every 4th row
until there are 13 sts between markers.
(53 sts)
Work 3 rows even, ending with Row 1
of CP.
Next row (RS): Work to first marker,
slip 13 gusset sts onto holder to be
worked later, dropping markers. Kfb
and work to end of row. (41 sts)
Cont to work in CP as set until hand
measures 6.5cm (2½ in) from top of
gusset, ending with a WS row.

SHAPE TOP
Row 1 (RS): P1, p2tog, p20, CP15,
p2tog tbl, p1. (39 sts)
Row 2 and all WS rows: Work even.
Row 3: P1, p2tog, p19, CP14,
p2tog tbl, p1. (37 sts)
Row 5: P1, p2tog, p13, p2tog tbl, p1,
p2tog, CP13, p2tog tbl, p1. (33 sts)
Change to 4.00mm (US 6) needles.
Row 7: P1, p2tog, p11, p2tog tbl, p1,
p2tog, p11, p2tog tbl, p1. (29 sts)

Row 9: P1, p2tog, p9, p2tog tbl, p1,
p2tog, p9, p2tog tbl, p1. (25 sts)
Row 11: P1, p2tog, p7, p2tog tbl, p1,
p2tog, p7, p2tog tbl, p1. (21 sts)
Row 12: Cast (bind) off knitwise.

THUMB
Finish thumb as on Right Mitten.

FINISHING
Sew thumb seams.
Working with RS
facing, sew side
and top seams.
Sew in all loose
ends.

DESIGNED BY

Eyelet Arm-Warmers

Long and elegant, a simple eyelet detail adorns the length of the arm-warmers for a spectacular look. They can also be knitted as mittens with just a few extra steps.

YARN

Rowan 4-ply Soft (100% merino wool), approx. 50g (1¾oz)/175m (191yd) per ball
One ball of Sooty 372

NEEDLES

Four 2.75mm (US 2) double-pointed needles (dpns)
Four 2.25mm (US 1) double-pointed needles (dpns)

EXTRAS

Two stitch markers (for full mittens)
Stitch holder (for full mittens)
Tapestry needle

TENSION (GAUGE)

28 sts and 36 rows = 10cm (4in) square measured over St st using
2.75mm (US 2) needles.

TO FIT

One size

SKILL LEVEL

Intermediate

SPECIAL ABBREVIATIONS

See page 254 for information on m1l and m1r.

RIGHT ARM-WARMER

Using 2.75mm (US 2) dpns, cast on 60 sts.

Round 1: Knit, dividing sts evenly across three dpns.

Round 2: Join for working in the round (being careful not to twist), knit.

Rounds 3–4: Knit.

Round 5: Purl.

Round 6: [Yo, k2tog] to end of round.

Round 7: Purl.

Rounds 8–11: Knit.

Round 12: Fold cast-on edge under and make hem by knitting tog the cast-on round and the active round as follows: using 2.25mm (US 1) needles, [pick up first cast-on st with right needle and place it on left needle, k2tog]; cont for entire round, picking up the next cast-on st and knitting it tog with next active st.

Rounds 13–15: Using 2.75mm (US 2) needles, knit.

Round 16: K2tog, knit to end of round.

Rounds 17–19: Knit.

Round 20: Knit to last 2 sts, ssk. (58 sts)

Round 21: Purl.

Round 22: [Yo, k2tog] to end of rnd.

Round 23: Purl.

Round 24: K2tog, knit to end of rnd.

Rounds 25–27: Knit.

Round 28: Knit to last 2 sts, ssk. (56 sts)

BEGIN PATTERNING

Round 29: K13, [k2tog, yo, k12] twice, k2tog, yo, k13.

Round 30: K12, [k2tog, yo, k1, yo, ssk, k9] twice, k2tog, yo, k1, yo, ssk, k11.

Round 31: Knit.

Round 32: K2tog, knit to end of rnd.

Rounds 33–35: Knit.

Round 36: Knit to last 2 sts, ssk. (54 sts)

Round 37: K5, [k2tog, yo, k12] three times, k2tog, yo, k5.

Round 38: K4, [k2tog, yo, k1, yo, ssk, k9] three times, k2tog, yo, k1, yo, ssk, k3.

Rounds 39–44: As Rounds 31–36. (52 sts)

Round 45: K11, [k2tog, yo, k12] twice, k2tog, yo, k11.

Round 46: K10, [k2tog, yo, k1, yo, ssk, k9] three times.

Rounds 47–52: As Rounds 31–36. (50 sts)

Round 53: K3, [k2tog, yo, k12] three times, k2tog, yo, k3.

Round 54: K2, [k2tog, yo, k1, yo, ssk, k9] three times, k2tog, yo, k1, yo, ssk, k1.

Rounds 55–60: As Rounds 31–36. (48 sts)

Round 61: K9, [k2tog, yo, k12] twice, k2tog, yo, k9.

Round 62: K8, [k2tog, yo, k1, yo, ssk, k9] twice, k2tog, yo, k1, yo, ssk, k7.

Rounds 63–68: As Rounds 31–36. (46 sts)

Round 69: Yo, k14 [k2tog, yo, k12] twice, k2, k2tog.

Round 70: K1, yo, ssk, k11 [k2tog, yo, k1, yo, ssk, k9] twice, k2, k2tog, yo.

Rounds 71–76: As Rounds 31–36. (44 sts)

Round 77: K7, [k2tog, yo, k12] twice, k2tog, yo, k7.

Round 78: K6, [k2tog, yo, k1, yo, ssk, k9] twice, k2tog, yo, k1, yo, ssk, k5.

Rounds 79–84: As Rounds 31–36. (42 sts)

FOR SHORTER LENGTH

Skip the next 16 rounds and go to the Upper Hand section.

FOR LONGER LENGTH

Round 85: Yo, k12 [k2tog, yo, k12] twice, k2tog.

Round 86: K1, yo, ssk, k9 [k2tog, yo, k1, yo, ssk, k9] twice, k2tog, yo.

Rounds 87–92: Knit.

Round 93: K6, [k2tog, yo, k12] twice, k2tog, yo, k6.

Round 94: K5, [k2tog, yo, k1, yo, ssk, k9] twice, k2tog, yo, k1, yo, ssk, k4.

Rounds 95–100: Knit.

UPPER HAND

Round 1: [K13, yo, k1, yo] three times. (48 sts)

Rounds 2–8: Knit.

Round 9: K6, [yo, k1, yo, k15] twice, yo, k1, yo, k9. (54 sts)

Rounds 10–16: Knit.

Round 17: [K17, yo, k1, yo] three times. (60 sts)
Rounds 18–19: Knit.

UPPER HAND HEM
Rounds 20–22: Knit.
Round 23: Purl.
Round 24: [Yo, k2tog] to end of rnd.
Round 25: Purl.
Rounds 26–28: Knit.
Round 29: Make hem by knitting together the back of Round 20 (three rounds before the first purl round) and the active round as follows: using 2.25mm (US 1) needles, [pick up the back of the first st of Round 20 with right needle and place it on left needle, k2tog]; cont for entire round, picking up the back of the next st of Round 20 and knitting it tog with next active st.

FOR FULL MITTENS
RIGHT HAND
Round 1: Using 2.75mm (US 2) needles, k40, PM, k10, PM, k10.
Round 2 (inc): Knit to first marker, SM, m1r, knit to next marker, m1l, SM, knit to end of rnd. (12 sts bet markers for thumb)
Round 3: Knit.
Round 4: As Round 2. (14 sts between markers)
Round 5: Knit.
Round 6: As Round 2. (16 sts between markers)

Round 7: Knit to first marker, remove marker, place 16 thumb sts onto stitch holder, remove second marker, cast 2 sts onto right needle, knit to end of rnd. Knit every round until mitten measures 11.5cm (4½ in) from thumb hole OR until it measures 3.5cm (1⅜ in) shorter than desired mitten length.

MITTEN TOP
Next round: K15, PM, k26, PM, k11.
Next round (dec): [Knit to 3 sts before marker, ssk, k1, SM, k1, k2tog] twice, knit to end of rnd.
Next round: Knit.
Rep last 2 rounds until 36 sts rem.
Rep only the dec rnd until 16 sts rem.
Next round: Knit to first marker, cut yarn leaving a 22.5cm (9in) tail. Place the 8 sts between markers on one needle; place the other 8 sts on a second needle. Sew tog using Kitchener st.

THUMB
(SAME FOR BOTH HANDS)
Place the 16 thumb sts on two 2.75mm (US 2) needles. With third needle, pick up and knit 4–6 sts (depending on how wide you would like the thumbs to be). Knit all rounds until thumb measures 5cm (2in), or desired length, from picked-up sts.
Next round: [K2tog] to end of rnd. (10 sts)
Next round: [K2tog] to end of rnd. (5 sts)

Cut yarn, leaving a 10cm (4in) tail. Thread tail through all rem sts and pull to close. Sew in all loose ends.

LEFT ARM-WARMER
Work as for Right Arm-Warmer to beginning of Right Hand.

LEFT HAND
Round 1: Using 2.75mm (US 2) needles, k10, PM, k10, PM, knit to end. Complete left hand as for right hand until Mitten Top.

MITTEN TOP
Next round: K11, PM, k26, PM, k15. Complete as for Right Hand.

FINGERLESS MITTENS
Work right and left hands as for Full Mittens until hand measures 7.5cm (3in) and thumb measures 2cm (⅞in) or just shorter than desired length. Finish hands and thumbs with the foll 4 rounds:
Next round: Purl.
Next round: [Yo, k2tog] to end of rnd.
Next round: Purl.
Using 2.25mm (US 1) needle, cast (bind) off.

DESIGNED BY

Sophie Britten

Bow Belles Mittens

These classic mittens, made in soft wool and cotton, are made in one piece and adorned with a contrasting whisper-soft ribbon.

YARN

Rowan Wool Cotton (50% merino wool, 50% cotton), approx. 50g (1¾oz)/113m (124yd) per ball
   One ball of Antique 900 (**MC**)
Rowan Kidsilk Haze (70% super kid mohair, 30% silk), approx. 25g (1oz)/210m (230yd) per ball
   Two balls of Candy Girl 606 (**A**)

NEEDLES

Pair of 4.00mm (US 6) knitting needles
One 4.00mm (US 6) circular needle
One 2.50mm (C/2) crochet hook

EXTRAS

Tapestry needle

TENSION (GAUGE)

Mittens: 23 sts and 29 rows = 10cm (4in) square measured over St st using 4.00mm (US 6) needles.
Ribbon: 26 sts and 28 rows = 10cm (4in) square measured over St st using 4.00mm (US 6) needles.

TO FIT

One size

SKILL LEVEL

Intermediate

SPECIAL ABBREVIATIONS

See pages 254–5 for information on m1l, m1r and three-needle cast (bind) off.

MITTENS (MAKE 2)

CUFF

Using 4.00mm (US 6) needles and MC, cast on 39 sts using Continental method.

Starting with a purl row, work 17 rows in St st, ending with a purl row.

PALM

Next row (RS): K3, m1l, k16, m1l, k1, m1r, k16, m1r, k3. (43 sts)

Next and all WS rows: Purl.

Next RS row: K3, m1l, k17, m1l, k3, m1r, k17, m1r, k3. (47 sts)

Next RS row: K21, m1l, k5, m1r, k21. (49 sts)

Next RS row: K21, m1l, k7, m1r, k21. (51 sts)

Next RS row: K21, m1l, k9, m1r, k21. (53 sts)

Next RS row: K21, m1l, k11, m1r, k21. (55 sts)

Purl 1 row.

THUMB

Row 1: K34, slip rem sts onto circular needle.

Row 2: P13, slip rem sts onto circular needle.

Rows 3–12: Work straight in St st.

Row 13: K1, [k2tog, k1] to end. (9 sts)

Row 14: Purl.

Row 15: [K2tog, k1] three times.

Slip all sts onto a crochet hook, wrap the yarn round the hook and draw through all sts on hook.

With RS facing, close thumb by working 1 row of slip stitch down side of thumb, inserting the hook into the RH strand of the edge stitch nearest you and into the LH strand of the back edge. Keep remaining loop on hook – this will be picked up in the next row.

HAND

With RS facing, return first 21 sts to straight needle, slip loop from crochet hook onto needle and knit across rest of row. (43 sts)

Next row: Purl.

Work 16 rows straight in St st.

Next RS row: K1, k2tog, k16, k2tog, k1, k2tog, k16, k2tog, k1. (39 sts)

Next and all WS rows: Purl.

Next RS row: K1, k2tog, k14, k2tog, k1, k2tog, k14, k2tog, k1. (35 sts)

Next RS row: K1, k2tog, k12, k2tog, k1, k2tog, k12, k2tog, k1. (31 sts)

Next RS row: K1, [k2tog, k1] to end. (21 sts)

Next RS row: [K1, k2tog] three times, k3, [k2tog, k1] three times. (15 sts)

Next row: P6, p2tog, slip last st back onto left needle, fold work in half with RS tog, so both needles are facing the same way with 7 sts on each needle. Work three-needle cast (bind) off (see page 255) until 1 loop remains on right needle, transfer loop to crochet hook and turn mittens right-side out. Slip stitch down the side seam, inserting the hook into the RH strand of the edge st

nearest you and into the LH strand of the back edge. Do not fasten off.

CUFF EDGE

Still using the crochet hook, work 1 round of dc (sc) into each st around bottom of cuff, slip stitch into first st. Fasten off.

RIBBONS (MAKE 2)

Using 4.00mm (US 6) needles and A, cast on 3 sts.
Working in St st, kfb at beg of next and every foll knit row until there are 12 sts.
Work straight st until ribbon measures 50cm (20in).
K2tog at beg of next and every foll knit row until 3 sts rem.
Cast (bind) off rem 3 sts purlwise.

FINISHING

Sew in all loose ends. Gently press all items. Wrap the ribbon around each mitten and tie in a bow, then arrange and sew ribbon in place on inner wrist.

THE END

If you don't want to finish the mitten in crochet, simply cut the yarn leaving a long tail and thread it through all the remaining loops, drawing them closed. Now sew down the side of the thumb/mitten, making an invisible seam. After you have sewn up the thumb, and slipped the first 21 sts back onto your needle, pick up a st where the thumb meets the palm in the following row. Be aware that the round of crochet around the bottom will stop the cuff from rolling up and into the bow.

DESIGNED BY

Firecracker Mitts

Expect fireworks when you wear these cracking mitts. The stylish pattern and super-soft wool yarn make them just right for city wear.

YARN

Rowan Scottish Tweed 4-ply (100% wool), approx.
25g (1oz)/110m (120yd) per ball
  One ball of Claret 013 **(A)**
  One ball of Brilliant Pink 010 **(B)**
Rowan Kidsilk Haze (70% super kid mohair, 30% silk), approx.
25g (1oz)/210m (229yd) per ball
  One ball of Marmalade 596 **(C)**
  One ball of Blueberry 600 **(D)**

NEEDLES

Pair of 4.00mm (US 6) knitting needles
Pair of 3.25mm (US 3) knitting needles

EXTRAS

Tapestry needle

TENSION (GAUGE)

22 sts and 30 rows = 10cm (4in) square measured over St st using 4.00mm (US 6) needles and Kidsilk Haze and Scottish Tweed together.

TO FIT

One size

SKILL LEVEL

Intermediate

MITTS (MAKE 2)

Using 3.25mm (US 3) needles and A and C tog, cast on 49 sts.

Row 1: K1, [p1, k1] to end.

Change to B and D tog.

Row 2: P1, [k1, p1] to end.

Row 3: K1, [p1, k1] to end.

Rep Rows 2–3 eight times more.

Change to 4.00mm (US 6) needles.

Row 20: Knit to last st, kfb. (50 sts)

Row 21: Purl.

Row 22: K2, [yfwd, k2tog, k2] to last 2 sts, k2.

Row 23: Purl.

Work from chart for 4 rows.

INCREASE FOR THUMB

Keeping patt correct:

Row 28: Work 23 sts from chart, kfb, work 2, kfb, pattern to end. (52 sts)

Row 29: Work 25 sts from chart, p2 using B and D only, work 25 sts to end. Use separate wrappings of yarns A and C for right and left sides. Thumb sts are knitted in yarns B and D only throughout.

Row 30: Work 25 sts, inc 1, k4, inc 1, work 25 sts. (54 sts)

Keeping patt correct, work from chart, increasing for thumb gusset as set in previous rows until 62 sts.

Next row (Row 16 of chart): Work 25 sts from chart, work 12 sts of thumb gusset, turn.

THUMB

Next row: P12, turn.

Working only these 12 sts, work a further 10 rows in St st, or until required length, ending with a purl row.

Next row: K1, [k2tog] to last st, k1.

Cut off yarn, leaving approx. 15–20cm (6–8in), thread through sts and draw together. Secure yarn and sew sides together.

Rejoining yarn, pick up 2 sts at base of thumb and complete Row 16 of chart.

Next row: Keeping patt correct, work 24 sts, [p2tog] twice, work to end. (50 sts)

Complete chart.

Work 6 rows in St st using yarns A and C only.

SHAPE TOP

Next row: K1, sl1, k1, psso, k20, k2tog, sl1, k1, psso, k20, k2tog, k1. (46 sts)

Work 3 rows in St st.

Next row: K1, sl1, k1, psso, k18, k2tog, sl1, k1, psso, k18, k2tog, k1. (42 sts)

Work 3 rows in St st.

Next row: K1, sl1, k1, psso, k16, k2tog, sl1, k1, psso, k16, k2tog, k1. (38 sts)

Next row: Purl.

Next row: K1, sl1, k1, psso, k16, k2tog, sl1, k1, psso, k16, k2tog, k1. (34 sts)

Next row: Purl.

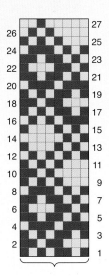

Key

□ A and C
■ B and D

Next row: K1, sl1, k1, psso, k14, k2tog, sl1, k1, psso, k14, k2tog, k1. (30 sts)

Cut off yarn.

FINISHING

Sew in all loose ends, then block and press. Sew up side seams using mattress stitch (see page 255), taking care to match up pattern. Make twisted cord and thread through eyelets.

FIRE-STARTER

Try exchanging the twisted cord for a silk ribbon or similar material to add a touch of elegance to the design.

DESIGNED BY

Melissa Halvorson

Sequined Mittens

Sparkly sequins lend a fun and playful touch to these sumptuous mohair mittens. Alternatively, an array of multicoloured beads is just as pretty.

YARN

Rowan Kidsilk Haze (70% super kid mohair, 30% silk), approx. 25g (1oz)/210m (229yd) per ball
   One ball of Splendour 579 **(A)**
Rowan Kid Classic (70% lambswool, 26% kid mohair, 4% nylon), approx. 50g (1¾oz)/140m (153yd) per ball
   One ball of Frilly 844 **(B)**

NEEDLES

Set of 5.00mm (US 8) double-pointed needles (dpns)

EXTRAS

Approx. 500 x 6mm (¼ in) sequins
Sewing needle and thread
Stitch holder
Two stitch markers
Tapestry needle

TENSION (GAUGE)

16 sts and 22 rows = 10cm (4in) square measured over St st using both yarns together.

TO FIT

One size

SKILL LEVEL

Beginner

DUPLICATE STITCH

Bring the threaded needle through the back just below the stitch you would like to cover. In one motion, pick up a sequin and insert the needle under both loops one row above and pull it through, anchoring the sequin to one side of the stitch. Pick up a second sequin and insert the needle back into the stitch below.

MITTENS (MAKE 2)

Using one strand of each yarn, cast on 30 sts and divide sts evenly across dpns. Join for working in the round, being careful not to twist. PM for start of round.

Round 1: [K2, p1] to end.
Work in k2, p1 rib for 10cm (4in) or desired length of gauntlet.
Next round: K to marker, SM, k2, PM.
Next round: K to marker (2 sts between markers).

THUMB GUSSET

Next round: SM, m1, k2, m1, SM, k to end. (4 sts between markers)
Knit 2 rounds.
Next round: SM, m1, k4, m1, SM, k to end.
Knit 2 rounds.
Cont in this manner, inc at each marker every 3rd round, until there are 12 sts between the markers.

Next round (to make up for 2 sts used for gusset): Knit to marker, m1, SM, k12 and place these 12 sts just worked onto a stitch holder, remove marker, m1.

PALM

Knit 10 rows.
Row 11: SM, k15, PM, k15.
Rows 12, 14, 16, 18, 20, 22: [Knit to 2 sts before marker, k2tog tbl, SM, k2tog] twice.
Rows 13, 15, 17, 19, 21: Knit.
When only 6 sts are left, thread yarn through twice in a clockwise motion and grip. Thread yarn through centre of the gripped stitches and pull inside.

THUMB

Pick up the 12 thumb sts with dpns, twisting the 2 sts closest to the join with the palm to prevent a gap.
Work in St st for 10 rows or desired length of thumb.
Row 11: [K2tog] to end. (6 sts)
Finish as for the top of the mitten.

FINISHING

Sew in all loose ends.
Apply sequins using duplicate stitch as described above.

DESIGNED BY

Lace Gloves

Lacy gloves with a touch of sparkle are perfect for eveningwear. A delicate diamanté button sits on the outside cuff to finish off the look.

YARN

Twilley's Goldfingering (80% viscose, 20% metallised polyester), approx. 50g (1¾oz)/200m (219yd) per ball
   Two balls of Ebony 31

NEEDLES

Pair of 3.00mm (US 2/3) knitting needles

EXTRAS

Two stitch markers
Two row markers
Tapestry needle
Sewing needle and thread
Two 10mm (½in) diameter buttons

TENSION (GAUGE)

28 sts and 38 rows = 10cm (4in) square measured over St st using 3.00mm (US 2/3) needles.

TO FIT

One size

SKILL LEVEL

Advanced

BEAD STITCH (BS)

Worked over multiple of 6 sts + 1 st.
This is a traditional Shetland lace
pattern, with every row knit.

Row 1: SM, k2, *yo, sl1, k2tog, psso,
yo, k3*; rep from * to * until 5 sts before
next marker, yo, sl1, k2tog, psso, yo, k2,
SM.

Row 2: SM, k1, k2tog, *yo, k1, yo,
k2tog, k1, k2tog*; rep from * to * until
4 sts before next marker, yo, k1, yo,
k2tog, k1, SM.

Row 3: SM, k2tog, yo, *k3, yo, sl1,
k2tog, psso, yo*; rep from * to * until
5 sts before next marker, k3, yo,
k2tog, SM.

Row 4: SM, k1, yo, k2tog, k1, *k2tog,
yo, k1, yo, k2tog, k1*; rep from * to *
until 3 sts before next marker, k2tog,
yo, k1, SM.

SEWN CHAIN STITCH LOOP

Secure a length of yarn to the edge of
the glove and thread tapestry needle.
Insert needle back in at the same point
and draw up to make a small loop.
Insert needle into this loop from
underneath, draw yarn through and
reinsert from on top. Gently tighten up
the first loop. Rep until chain is desired
length to accommodate the button.
Fasten to glove edge, forming a loop.

LEFT GLOVE
PEPLUM

Cast on 10 sts. Work 3 rows in
garter stitch (knit every row).

Lace row 1 (RS): K4, yo, sl1, k2tog,
psso, yo, k3.

Lace row 2: K2, k2tog, yo, k1, yo,
k2tog, k3.

Lace row 3: K2, k2tog, yo, k3, yo,
k2tog, k1.

Lace row 4: K2, yo, k2tog, k1, k2tog,
yo, k3.

Rep the last 4 rows twenty-three times
more and the first row once more,
ending with WS facing.

Knit 3 rows, ending with RS facing.

Cast (bind) off 9 sts; 1 st now rem
on RH needle.

Pick up and knit 53 sts (approx. 1 st
every 2 rows) along nearest (LH) edge
of peplum. (54 sts)

THUMB GUSSET

Inc row (WS): K2, PM, k3, [kfb, k5]
four times, PM (31 sts between
markers), kfb, k11, kfb, k12. (60 sts)

Row 1 (RS): K25, m1, k2; work
BS Row 1, rep from * to * four times;
k2. (61 sts)

Row 2: K2; work BS Row 2,
rep from * to * four times, p to last
2 sts, k2.

Cont as established:

Row 3: K28, work BS Row 3, k2.

Row 4: K2, work BS Row 4, p to last
2 sts, k2.

Row 5: K25, m1, k3, work BS Row 1,
k2. (62 sts)

Row 6: As Row 2.

Row 7: K29, work BS Row 3, k2.

**Row 8 (mark both ends of this
row):** K2, PM, work BS Row 4, PM,
p to last 2 sts, k2. (62 sts)

Row 9: K25, m1, k8, m1, k2, PM;
work BS Row 1, rep from * to * twice;
PM, k8. (64 sts)

Row 10: P8; work BS Row 2,
rep from * to * twice; purl to end of row.

Row 11: Knit to marker, work
BS Row 3, k8.

Row 12: P8, work BS Row 4, p to end
of row.

Row 13: K25, m1, k10, m1, k2, work
BS Row 1, k8. (66 sts)

Rows 14–16: As Rows 10–12.

Row 17: K25, m1, k12, m1, k2, work
BS Row 1, k8. (68 sts)

Rows 18–20: As Rows 10–12.

Row 21: K25, m1, k14, m1, k2, work
BS Row 1, k8. (70 sts)

Rows 22–24: As Rows 10–12,
removing both markers on the last row.

THUMB

Next row: K41, turn, cast on 3 sts.

Next row: P19, turn, cast on 3 sts.

Starting with a knit row, work 20 rows
in St st on these 22 sts.

SHAPE TOP

Next row: K1, [k2tog, k2] to last st,
k1. (17 sts)

Next row: Purl.

Next row: K1, [k2tog] to end. (9 sts)

Cut off yarn, thread through rem sts,
draw up and fasten off.

Sew seam.

MAIN SECTION

Row 1: With RS facing, rejoin yarn, pick up and knit 5 sts at base of thumb, k10, yo, sl1, k2tog, psso, yo, knit to end of row. (59 sts)

Row 2: P14, k1, k2tog, yo, k1, yo, k2tog, k1, p10, p2tog, purl to end of row. (58 sts)

Row 3: K37, k2tog, yo, k3, yo, k2tog, knit to end of row.

Row 4: P14, k1, yo, k2tog, k1, k2tog, yo, k1, purl to end of row.

Row 5: K39, yo, sl1, k2tog, psso, yo, knit to end of row.

Row 6: P14, k1, k2tog, yo, k1, yo, k2tog, k1, purl to end of row.

Row 7: As Main Section Row 3.

Row 8: As Main Section Row 4.

Rep the last 4 rows.

DIVIDE FOR FOURTH FINGER

Next row: K39, yo, sl1, k2tog, psso, yo, k9, turn (7 sts rem unworked), cast on 2 sts.

Next row: P9, k1, k2tog, yo, k1, yo, k2tog, k1, p30, turn (7 sts rem unworked), cast on 2 sts.

Next row: K32, k2tog, yo, k3, yo, k2tog, k9, turn.

Next row: P9, k1, yo, k2tog, k1, k2tog, yo, k1, p32, turn.

FINGERS

FIRST FINGER

Next row: K32, turn, cast on 2 sts.

Next row: P18, turn, cast on 2 sts. (20 sts)

On these 20 sts only, work a further 22 rows in St st.

SHAPE TOP

Next row: K1, [k2tog, k2] to last 3 sts, k2tog, k1. (15 sts)

Next row: Purl.

Next row: K1, [k2tog] to end of row. (8 sts)

Cut off yarn, thread through rem sts, draw up and fasten off.

Sew seam.

SECOND FINGER

Row 1: With RS facing, pick up and knit 3 sts from base of first finger, k2, yo, sl1, k2tog, psso, yo, k2, turn, cast on 2 sts.

Row 2: P2, k1, k2tog, yo, k1, yo, k2tog, k1, p1, p2tog, p7, turn, cast on 2 sts. (20 sts)

Cont on these 20 sts as foll:

Row 3: K11, k2tog, yo, k3, yo, k2tog, k2.

Row 4: P2, k1, yo, k2tog, k1, k2tog, yo, k1, p11.

Row 5: K13, yo, sl1, k2tog, psso, yo, k4.

Row 6: P2, k1, k2tog, yo, k1, yo, k2tog, k1, p11.

Row 7: As Row 3.

Row 8: As Row 4.

Rep last 4 rows five times more.

SHAPE TOP

Work as for first finger.

Cut off yarn, thread through rem sts, draw up and fasten off.

Sew seam.

THIRD FINGER

Row 1: With RS facing, rejoin yarn, pick up and knit 3 sts from base of second finger, k9, turn.

Next row: P10, p2tog, p9, turn. (20 sts)

On these 20 sts only, work a further 22 rows in St st.

SHAPE TOP

As for first finger.

Cut off yarn, thread through rem sts, draw up and fasten off.

Sew seam.

FOURTH FINGER

Next row: With RS facing, rejoin yarn, pick up and knit 3 sts from base of third finger, knit to end of row. (17 sts)

Starting with a purl row, work 17 rows in St st.

SHAPE TOP

Next row: K1, [k2tog, k2] to end. (13 sts)

Next row: Purl.

Next row: K1, [k2tog] to end. (7 sts)

Cut off yarn, thread through rem sts, draw up and fasten off.

Sew side seam as far as the garter st edge (at the row markers).

RIGHT GLOVE

PEPLUM
Work as for Left Glove.

THUMB GUSSET
Inc row (WS): K12, kfb, k11, kfb, PM, k5, [kfb, k5] four times. (60 sts)
Row 1 (RS): K2, PM; work BS Row 1, rep from * to * four times; k2, m1, k25. (61 sts)
Row 2: K2, p26; work BS Row 2, rep from * to * four times; k2.
Row 3: K2, work BS Row 3, k28.
Row 4: K2, p26, work BS Row 4, k2.
Row 5: K2, work BS Row 1, k3, m1, k25. (62 sts)
Row 6: K2, p27, work BS Row 2, k2.
Row 7: K2, work BS Row 3, k29.
Row 8: K2, p27, work BS Row 4 and remove markers, k2.
Row 9: K8, PM; work BS Row 1, rep from * to * twice and ignoring references to markers; PM, k2, m1, k8, m1, k25. (64 sts)
Row 10: Purl to first marker; work BS Row 2, rep from * to * twice; p8.
Row 11: K8, PM, work BS Row 3, knit to end.
Row 12: Purl to first marker, work BS Row 4, p8.
Row 13: K8, work BS row 1, k2, m1, k10, m1, knit to end. (66 sts)
Rows 14–16: As Rows 10–12.
Row 17: K8, work BS Row 1, k2, m1, k12, m1, knit to end. (68 sts)
Rows 18–20: As Rows 10–12.

Row 21: K8, work BS Row 1, k2, m1, k14, m1, knit to end. (70 sts)
Rows 22–24: As Rows 10–12, removing markers on last row.

THUMB
Next row: K16, yo, sl1, k2tog, psso, yo, k26, turn, cast on 3 sts.
Next row: P19, turn, cast on 3 sts. (22 sts)
Starting with a knit row, work 20 rows in St st on these 22 sts.

SHAPE TOP
Next row: K1, [k2tog, k2] to last st, k1. (17 sts)
Next row: Purl.
Next row: K1, [k2tog] to end of row. (9 sts)
Cut off yarn, thread through rem sts, draw up and fasten off.
Sew side seam.

MAIN SECTION
Row 1: With RS facing, rejoin yarn, pick up and knit 5 sts at base of thumb, knit to end of row. (59 sts)
Row 2: P26, p2tog, p9, k1, k2tog, yo, k1, yo, k2tog, k1, purl to end of row. (58 sts)
Row 3: K14, k2tog, yo, k3, yo, k2tog, knit to end of row.
Row 4: P37, k1, yo, k2tog, k1, k2tog, yo, k1, purl to end of row.
Row 5: K16, yo, sl1, k2tog, psso, yo, knit to end of row.

Row 6: P37, k1, k2tog, yo, k1, yo, k2tog, k1, purl to end of row.
Row 7: As Main Section Row 3.
Row 8: As Main Section Row 4.
Rep the last 4 rows.

DIVIDE FOR FOURTH FINGER
Next row: K16, yo, sl1, k2tog, psso, yo, k32, turn (7 sts rem unworked), cast on 2 sts.
Next row: P32, k1, k2tog, yo, k1, yo, k2tog, k1, p7, turn (7 sts rem unworked), cast on 2 sts.
Next row: K9, k2tog, yo, k3, yo, k2tog, k32, turn.
Next row: P32, k1, yo, k2tog, k1, k2tog, yo, k1, p9, turn.

FINGERS

FIRST FINGER
Next row: K11, yo, sl1, k2tog, psso, yo, k18, turn, cast on 2 sts.
Next row: P18, turn, cast on 2 sts.
On these 20 sts only, work 22 rows in St st.

SHAPE TOP
Work as for Left Glove first finger.

SECOND FINGER
Row 1: With RS facing, rejoin yarn, pick up and knit 3 sts from base of first finger, k7, turn, cast on 2 sts.
Row 2: P9, p2tog, p1, k1, k2tog, yo, k1, yo, k2tog, k1, turn, cast on 2 sts.

Cont on these 20 sts as foll:
Row 3: K2, k2tog, yo, k3, yo, k2tog, k11.
Row 4: P11, k1, yo, k2tog, k1, k2tog, yo, k1, p2.
Row 5: K4, yo, sl1, k2tog, psso, yo, k13.

Row 6: P11, k1, k2tog, yo, k1, yo, k2tog, k1, p2.
Row 7: As Row 3.
Row 8: As Row 4.
Rep the last 4 rows five times more.

SHAPE TOP
As for Left Glove first finger.

THIRD FINGER
Work as for Left Glove third finger.

FOURTH FINGER
As for Left Glove fourth finger.

FINISHING
Sew in all loose ends.
Spray lightly with water and allow to dry thoroughly.
Sew or crochet a chain stitch loop at wrist (where peplum attaches to glove). Sew a button on edge of palm side of each glove to correspond with the loop – it is easier to do this with sewing thread rather than using the yarn.

SHAPE UP

- Work the last row of shaping for the thumb and fingers tightly or with a finer needle.
- For fingerless gloves, work 4 rows of the thumb and fingers, then cast (bind) off.

Hats

Whatever hat style you love — whether that's the Inca Hat, perfect for chilly days, or the Paris Beret, perfect to pair with any outfit, elegant or casual (and great for hiding a bad hair day!) — there's something here for you to make. Don't worry if you like the style but not the colour. Simply customise the pattern by using a colour palette that will accent your wardrobe or skin tone and make a perfectly unique hat for your head.

DESIGNED BY

Tweedy Cloche

Sweet and neat, this crochet cloche is worked in a felted yarn that is soft and easy to wear. The contrast brim adds a vivid colour accent, which is echoed in the simple bead detailing on the front.

YARN

Rowan Felted Tweed DK (50% merino wool, 25% alpaca, 25% viscose), approx. 50g (1¾oz)/175m (191yd) per ball
   One ball of Ginger 154 **(A)**
Rowan Pure Wool DK (100% superwash wool), approx. 50g (1¾oz)/125m (137yd) per ball
   One ball of Tea Rose 025 **(B)**

HOOKS

One 5.50mm (I/9) crochet hook
One 6.00mm (J/10) crochet hook

EXTRAS

Two 15mm (⅝in) clear pink faceted glass beads
Tapestry Needle

TENSION (GAUGE)

8 sts and 9 rows = 10cm (4in) square measured over double (single) crochet fabric using 6.00mm (J/10) hook and two strands of A held together.

TO FIT

One size

SKILL LEVEL

Intermediate

CLOCHE

Using 6.00mm (J/10) hook and two strands of A held together, make 3 ch and join with ss (sl st) to form a ring.

Round 1: 1 ch (does NOT count as st), 9 dc (sc) into ring, ss (sl st) to first dc (sc). (9 sts)

Round 2: 1 ch (does NOT count as st), 2 dc (sc) into each dc (sc) to end, ss (sl st) to first dc (sc). (18 sts)

Round 3: 1 ch (does NOT count as st), *1 dc (sc) into next dc (sc), 2 dc (sc) into next dc (sc); rep from * to end, ss (sl st) to first dc (sc). (27 sts).

Round 4: 1 ch (does NOT count as st), *1 dc (sc) into each of next 2 dc (sc), 2 dc (sc) into next dc (sc); rep from * to end, ss (sl st) to first dc (sc). (36 sts)

Round 5: 1 ch (does NOT count as st), *1 dc (sc) into each of next 3 dc (sc), 2 dc (sc) into next dc (sc); rep from * to end, ss (sl st) to first dc (sc). (45 sts)

Round 6: 1 ch (does NOT count as st), *1 dc (sc) into each of next 4 dc (sc), 2 dc (sc) into next dc (sc); rep from * to end, ss (sl st) to first dc (sc). (54 sts)

Round 7: 1 ch (does NOT count as st), *1 dc (sc) into each of next 8 dc (sc), 2 dc (sc) into next dc (sc); rep from * to end, ss (sl st) to first dc (sc). (60 sts)

Round 8: 1 ch (does NOT count as st), *1 dc (sc) into each of next 9 dc (sc), 2 dc (sc) into next dc (sc); rep from * to end, ss (sl st) to first dc (sc). (66 sts)

Round 9: 1 ch (does NOT count as st), 1 dc (sc) into each dc (sc) to end, ss (sl st) to first dc (sc).

Rounds 10–15: As round 9.

Round 16: 1 ch (does NOT count as st), *1 dc (sc) into each of next 10 dc (sc), miss next dc (sc); rep from * to end, ss (sl st) to first dc (sc). (60 sts)

Round 17: As round 9.

Round 18: 1 ch (does NOT count as st), *1 dc (sc) into each of next 9 dc (sc), miss next dc (sc); rep from * to end, ss (sl st) to first dc (sc). (54 sts)

Round 19: As round 9.

Round 20: 1 ch (does NOT count as st), *1 dc (sc) into each of next 8 dc (sc), miss next dc (sc); rep from * to end, ss (sl st) to first dc (sc). (48 sts)

Round 21: As round 9.

Cut off A and join in B.

Change to 5.50mm (I/9) hook.

Round 22: 1 ch (does NOT count as st), 2 dc (sc) into each dc (sc) to end, ss (sl st) to first dc (sc). (96 sts)

Rounds 23–26: As round 9.

Fasten off.

FINISHING

Sew in all loose ends, then block and press. Attach beads as in photograph.

FRAMED!

As the brim of the cloche will frame your face, work it in a yarn colour to complement your skin tone. If you are dark-skinned, then the bright pink shown will be perfect. For an olive skin, consider a turquoise or lilac colour. If you are pale-skinned, then a fresh green or a soft grey will look great.

DESIGNED BY

Fair Isle Beret

Working traditional Fair Isle patterns in contemporary colours gives them a fresh twist that fits in perfectly with today's vintage fashions. This is also a great hat for bad hair days, as it's big enough to tuck away frizzy curls and bed-head locks.

YARN

Rowan Pure Wool DK (100% superwash wool), approx. 50g (1¾oz)/125m (137yd) per ball

One ball of Hay 014 **(A)**
One ball of Barley 015 **(B)**
One ball of Avocado 019 **(C)**
One ball of Shale 002 **(D)**
One ball of Damson 030 **(E)**
One ball of Kiss 036 **(F)**
One ball of Glade 021 **(G)**

NEEDLES

Pair of 3.25mm (US 3) knitting needles
Pair of 4.00mm (US 6) knitting needles

EXTRAS

Tapestry Needle

TENSION (GAUGE)

24 sts and 32 rows = 10cm (4in) square measured over patt using 4.00mm (US 6) needles.

TO FIT

One size

SKILL LEVEL

Intermediate

LOVE THIS? Try knitting the Fair Isle Tote by Fiona on page 208.

BERET

Using 3.25mm (US 3) needles and A, cast on 108 sts.

Row 1 (RS): [K1, p1] to end.

Row 2: As Row 1.

These 2 rows form rib.

Cont in rib for 7 rows more, ending with a RS row.

Row 10 (WS): Rib 1, m1, rib 1, [m1, rib 2] to end. (162 sts)

Change to 4.00mm (US 6) needles.

Repeating the 8-st patt rep 20 times across each row and working first and last sts as indicated, work in St st from chart as follows:

Work chart rows 1–18, ending with a WS row.

Row 19 (RS): With A, k1, [m1, k8] to last st, k1. (182 sts)

Row 20: [With E p1, with A p1] to end.

Row 21: [With E k1, with A k1] to end.

Row 22: With A, purl.

Row 23: With A, k1, [skpo, k7] to last st, k1. (162 sts)

Work chart rows 24–28.

Row 29 (RS): With A, k1, [skpo, k8] to last st, k1. (146 sts)

Row 30: With A, purl.

Repeating the 8-st patt rep 18 times across each row and working first and last sts as indicated, work in St st from chart as follows:

Work chart rows 1–2, ending with a WS row.

Row 33 (RS): With A, k1, [skpo, k7] to last st, k1. (130 sts)

Repeating the 8-st patt rep 16 times across each row and working first and last sts as indicated, work in St st from chart as follows:

Work chart rows 4–16, ending with a WS row.

Row 47 (RS): With A k1, with G k1, [with A skpo, k1, with G k1] to end. (98 sts)

Row 48: With A, purl.

Row 49: With A, k1, [skpo] to last st, k1. (50 sts)

Rows 50–51: As Rows 20–21.

Row 52: With A, p1, [p2tog tbl] to last st, p1. (26 sts)

Row 53: As Row 49.

Break off yarn and thread through rem 14 sts. Pull up tight and fasten off securely.

FINISHING

Sew in all loose ends, then block and press. Join back seam.

FADE TO GREY

For a striking, graphic look, you could work this beret with a white background and replace the colours with black and shades of grey and slate blue. To do this you'll almost definitely have to use yarns from different ranges to get the right colours, and this is fine as long as the tension (gauge) of each is similar. Collect together all the yarns you want to use and check that the average tensions (gauges) given on the ball bands are all similar, both to each other and to the project tension (gauge) – a stitch or row different either way is fine. Knit a tension (gauge) swatch in the Fair Isle pattern and measure it carefully before you start your hat.

Key

- A
- B
- C
- D
- E
- F
- G

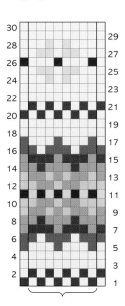

DESIGNED BY

Elizabethan Beret

Classic colours and historical inspiration combine to make a deliciously pretty beret that'll look perfect at any event, be it a winter wedding or summer party. Team it with a white wool coat or black and white floral print dress.

YARN

Rowan Cashcotton DK (35% cotton, 25% polyamide, 18% angora, 13% viscose, 9% cashmere), approx. 50g (1¾oz)/130m (142yd) per ball
- One ball of White 600 **(A)**
- One ball of Black 607 **(B)**

NEEDLES

Set of four 3.25mm (US 3) double-pointed needles (dpns)
Set of four 4.00mm (US 6) double-pointed needles (dpns)
One 3.25mm (D/3) crochet hook

EXTRAS

75cm (29½ in) of 7cm (2¾ in) wide black lace
Sewing needle and black thread
One 6mm (¼ in) silver pearl bead
Tapestry needle

TENSION

22 sts and 30 rows = 10cm (4in) square measured over St st using 4.00mm (US 6) needles.

TO FIT

One size

SKILL LEVEL

Intermediate

LOVE THIS? Try knitting the Black and White Evening Bag by Sue on page 212.

BERET

Using 3.25mm (US 3) needles and B, cast on 120 sts. Divide sts evenly across three dpns; join for working in the round.

Rounds 1–8: [K2, p2] to end.

Round 9: [Rib 4, kfb] to end. (144 sts) Cut off B and join in A.

Rounds 10–36: Knit.

Round 37: K2tog, k15, [sl1, k2tog, psso, k15] to last st, slip last st and then pass this slipped st over first st of round (at beg of next round). (128 sts)

Rounds 38–39: Knit.

Round 40: K2tog, k13, [sl1, k2tog, psso, k13] to last st, slip last st and then pass this slipped st over first st of round (at beg of next round). (112 sts)

Rounds 41–42: Knit.

Round 43: K2tog, k11, [sl1, k2tog, psso, k11] to last st, slip last st and then pass this slipped st over first st of round (at beg of next round). (96 sts)

Rounds 44–45: Knit.

Round 46: K2tog, k9, [sl1, k2tog, psso, k9] to last st, slip last st and then pass this slipped st over first st of round (at beg of next round). (80 sts)

Rounds 47–48: Knit.

Round 49: K2tog, k7, [sl1, k2tog, psso, k7] to last st, slip last st and then pass this slipped st over first st of round (at beg of next round). (64 sts)

Rounds 50–51: Knit.

Round 52: K2tog, k5, [sl1, k2tog, psso, k5] to last st, slip last st and then pass this slipped st over first st of round (at beg of next round). (48 sts)

Round 53: Knit.

Round 54: K2tog, k3, [sl1, k2tog, psso, k3] to last st, slip last st and then pass this slipped st over first st of round (at beg of next round) (32 sts).

Round 55: Knit.

Round 56: K2tog, k1, [sl1, k2tog, psso, k1] to last st, slip last st and then pass this slipped st over first st of round (at beg of next round). (16 sts)

Rounds 57–58: Knit.

Cut off yarn and thread through rem 16 sts. Pull up tight and fasten off securely.

FLOWER

Using 3.25mm (D/3) crochet hook and B, make 6 ch and join with ss (sl st) to form a ring.

Round 1: 1 ch (does NOT count as st), 1 dc (sc) into ring, [1 tr (dc), 1 dtr (tr), 4 ch and 1 dc (sc) into ring] six times, replacing dc (sc) at end of last rep with ss (sl st) to first dc (sc). (6 petals)

Round 2: [4 ch (keeping this ch behind petals of prev round), 1 ss (sl st) into next dc (sc)] six times, working last ss (sl st) into same place as ss (sl st) at end of prev round.

Round 3: 1 ch (does NOT count as st), [1 dc (sc), 1 tr (dc), 1 dtr (tr), 4 ch, 1 dc (sc), 1 tr (dc), 1 dtr (tr), 4 ch and 1 dc (sc)] into each ch sp to end, ss (sl st) to first dc (sc). (12 petals)

Round 4: [5 ch (keeping this ch behind petals of prev round), miss 1 dc (sc), 1 ss (sl st) into next dc (sc)] six times, working last ss (sl st) into same place as ss (sl st) at end of prev round.

Cut off B and join in A.

Round 5: 1 ch (does NOT count as st), [1 dc (sc), 8 ch, 1 dc (sc) and 8 dc (sc)] into each ch sp to end, replacing '8 ch' at end of last rep with '4 ch, 1 tr (dc) into first dc (sc)'. (12 ch sps)

Round 6: 3 ch (counts as first tr (dc)), 1 tr (dc) into ch sp partly formed by tr (dc) at end of prev round, *4 ch, [2 tr (dc), 2 ch and 2 tr (dc)] into next ch sp; rep from *, ending 4 ch, 2 tr (dc) into same ch sp as used at beg of round, 2 ch, ss (sl st) to top of 3 ch at beg of round.

Round 7: 1 ch (does NOT count as st), 1 dc (sc) into st at base of 1 ch, 1 dc (sc) into next tr (dc), *[2 dc (sc), 6 ch and 2 dc (sc)] into next ch sp, 1 dc (sc) into each of next 2 tr (dc), 2 dc (sc) into next ch sp**, 1 dc (sc) into each of next 2 tr (dc); rep from *, ending last rep at **, ss (sl st) to first dc (sc).

Fasten off.

FINISHING

Sew in all loose ends, then block and press. Join ends of lace. Using photograph as a guide, neatly sew lace to Beret, positioning lace just above rib section in B – ensure lace is sewn on so that Beret will still stretch enough to fit onto head. Attach Flower to Beret as in photograph, attaching the pearl bead in the centre.

COLOUR PLAY

This beret would also look fabulous knitted in a strong colour, such as deep turquoise, and trimmed with cotton lace in a lighter shade of the same colour. As yarn is available in such a wide range of colours and lace in a smaller range, it may be best to pick the lace first and then find a yarn to go with it.

DESIGNED BY

Be Seen Beret

This pillbox-style beret is a real scene stealer. Worked in the finest cashmere yarn on slender needles, it isn't the quickest hat to make, but the end result is worth every second of work.

YARN

Jade Sapphire 2-ply Mongolian Cashmere (100% pure cashmere), approx. 55g (2oz)/365m (399yd) per skein

   One skein of Cousin Coral 058

NEEDLES

Set of four 2.00mm (US 0) double-pointed needles (dpns)

EXTRAS

Small amount of waste yarn (for cast on)

Eight stitch markers

Tapestry needle

TENSION (GAUGE)

36 sts and 52 rows = 10cm (4in) square measured over patt using 2.00mm (US 0) needles.

TO FIT

One size

SKILL LEVEL

Advanced

SPECIAL ABBREVIATIONS

See page 254 for information on PK.

BERET

With waste yarn, cast on 208 sts. Divide sts evenly across three dpns; join for working in the round.

Round 1: Knit.

Cut off waste yarn and join in main yarn.

CROWN SECTION

Round 1: [K26, PM] eight times.

Round 2: [Knit to within 2 sts of M, k2tog, SM to RH needle] eight times. (200 sts)

Round 3: [Knit to marker, SM to RH needle] eight times.

Working MK at random over St st sections, rep last 2 rounds 24 times more.

Break off yarn and thread through rem 8 sts. Pull up tight and fasten off securely.

LOWER SECTION

Carefully unravel waste yarn at cast-on edge and slip the 208 sts of first round in main yarn onto dpns.

Join in main yarn and, working downwards from crown section, cont as follows:

Round 1: P1, knit to end.

Round 2: Purl.

Round 3: As Round 1.

Round 4: [P24, p2tog] eight times. (200 sts)

Round 5: Knit to end, winding yarn round needle twice for each st.

Round 6: *Slip next 4 sts onto RH needle, dropping extra loops, slip same 4 sts back onto LH needle, p4tog leaving sts on LH needle, now work (k1, p1, k1) into same 4 sts and let all 4 sts fall from LH needle; rep from * to end.

Rounds 7–9: As Rounds 1–3.

Round 10: [P23, p2tog] eight times. (192 sts)

Rounds 11–12: As Rounds 5–6.

Rounds 13–15: As Rounds 1–3.

Round 16: [P22, p2tog] eight times. (184 sts)

Rounds 17–18: As Rounds 5–6.

Rounds 19–22: Rep Rounds 1–2 twice.

Rounds 23–30: [K1, p1] to end.

Cast (bind) off in rib.

FINISHING

Sew in all loose ends, then block and press.

ALL THAT GLITTERS

You could knit this hat in a fine crochet yarn, which is available in many colours including some fantastic metallics. Do work a tension (gauge) swatch and check the stitch and row counts carefully before you start the project or you may discover that after all that work your new hat really doesn't fit. A little tassel made as for the one on the Beaded Beret (page 106) could be sewn to the top of this beret as a finishing touch.

DESIGNED BY

Lace Snood

The perfect combination of pretty and practical, this snood will keep you cosy and looking good. Make it a permanent fixture in your handbag during the winter months and whip it out when the wind blows.

YARN

Rowan Damask (57% viscose, 22% linen, 21% acrylic), approx. 50g (1¾oz)/ 105m (115yd) per ball

   Two balls of Mica 040

NEEDLES

Pair of 3.75mm (US 5) knitting needles

EXTRAS

Stitch holder

Tapestry needle

TENSION (GAUGE)

24 sts and 29 rows = 10cm (4in) square measured over St st using 3.75mm (US 5) needles.

TO FIT

One size

SKILL LEVEL

Intermediate

SNOOD

Cast on 123 sts.
Row 1 (RS): K1, [p1, k1] to end.
Row 2: P1, [k1, p1] to end.
These 2 rows form rib.
Cont in rib until work measures
14cm (5½ in), ending with a WS row.
Next row (RS): K1, p1, *k3tog,
[p1, k1] twice, p1; rep from * to last st,
k1. (93 sts)
Cont in rib until work measures
16cm (6¼in), ending with a WS row.
Cast (bind) off 14 sts at beg of next
2 rows. (65 sts)
Now work in lace patt as follows:
Row 1 (RS): P2, [k5, p2] to end.
Row 2: K2, [p5, k2] to end.
Row 3: P2, [k2tog, yfwd, k1, yfwd,
skpo, p2] to end.
Row 4: As row 2.
These 4 rows form lace patt.
Cont in lace patt until work measures
27cm (10½ in) from cast-on edge,
ending with a WS row.
Keeping patt correct, cast (bind) off
16 sts at beg of next 2 rows. (33 sts)
Cont straight in patt until work measures
10cm (4in) from cast-off (bound-off) sts,
ending with a WS row.
Cut yarn and leave rem 33 sts on
a holder.
Sew row-end edges of last 10cm (4in)
to cast-off (bound-off) sts.

BORDER

With RS facing, pick up and knit 14 sts
along first cast-off (bound-off) edge
of rib section, and 22 sts up row-end
edge, patt across 33 sts on holder,
pick up and knit 22 sts down other
row-end edge, then 14 sts along other
cast-off (bound-off) edge. (105 sts)
Starting with row 2, work in rib as given
for lower edge for 11 rows, ending with
a WS row.
Cast (bind) off in rib.

FINISHING

Sew in all loose ends, then block
and press.
Sew centre front chin seam using
mattress stitch (see page 255).

DESIGNED BY

Tweed Cap

Making the most of self-striping yarn, this cap also uses a stitch-weaving pattern that creates a firm knitted fabric so the cap holds its shape. Wear your cap with skinny jeans and an oversized, chunky jumper or a long leather coat.

YARN

Twilley's Freedom Spirit (100% pure new wool), approx. 50g (1¾oz)/120m (131yd) per ball
 Three balls of Essence 507 **(A)**
Twilley's Freedom Wool (100% pure new wool), approx. 50g (1¾oz)/50m (54yd) per ball
 One ball of Navy 423 **(B)**

NEEDLES

Pair of 6.50mm (US 10½) knitting needles
Set of four 6.50mm (US 10½) double-pointed needles (dpns)
One 3.75mm (F/5) crochet hook

EXTRAS

Piece of buckram 12cm by 30cm (4¾in by 11¾in)
One 25mm (1in) diameter self-cover button
70cm (27½in) of 12mm (½in) wide satin ribbon
Sewing needle and thread
Tapestry needle

TENSION (GAUGE)

25 sts and 34 rows = 10cm (4in) square measured over patt using 6.50mm (US 10½) needles and A.

TO FIT

One size

SKILL LEVEL

Intermediate

CROWN PANELS (MAKE 6)

Using 6.50mm (US 10½) needles and A, cast on 25 sts.

Row 1 (RS): K1, *bring yarn to front (RS) of work, slip next st purlwise, take yarn to back (WS) of work, k1; rep from * to end.

Row 2: Sl1, *p1, take yarn to back (RS) of work, slip next st purlwise, bring yarn to front (WS) of work; rep from * to end.

These 2 rows form patt.

Cont in patt, kfb at each end of next and 2 foll 8th rows, taking inc sts into patt. (31 sts)

Work 9 rows, ending with a WS row. Keeping patt correct, dec 1 st at each end of next and 4 foll 4th rows, then on foll 9 alt rows, ending with a RS row.

Next row (WS): P3tog and fasten off.

BAND AND PEAK

Matching fasten-off points of all six sections at centre of crown, sew Crown Panels together along row-end edges, leaving cast-on edges free.

Starting at one seam, using 6.50mm (US 10½) dpns and A, with RS facing pick up and knit 143 sts around cast-on edge of Crown Panels (this is 24 sts for the first five sections and 23 sts for the sixth section). Divide sts evenly across three dpns and work in rounds as follows:

Round 1: K1, *bring yarn to front (RS) of work, slip next st purlwise, take yarn to back (WS) of work, k1; rep from * to end.

Round 2: *Bring yarn to front (RS) of work, slip next st purlwise, take yarn to back (WS) of work, k1; rep from * to last st, bring yarn to front (RS) of work, slip next st purlwise, take yarn to back (WS) of work.

These 2 rounds form patt.

Work 5 rounds more – band section completed.

SHAPE PEAK

**Keeping patt correct (by working patt as given for Crown Panels) and working backwards and forwards in short rows, shape peak as follows:

Rows 1–2: Patt 2 sts, turn.
Row 3 (RS): Patt 4 sts, turn.
Row 4: Patt 2 sts, turn.
Rows 5–6: Patt 6 sts, turn.
Row 7: Skpo, patt 6 sts, turn.
Row 8: Patt 8 sts, turn.
Rows 9–10: Patt 9 sts, turn.
Row 11: Skpo, patt 9 sts, turn.
Row 12: Patt 10 sts, turn.
Rows 13–14: Patt 13 sts, turn.
Row 15: Skpo, patt 14 sts, turn.
Row 16: Patt 15 sts, turn.
Row 17: Skpo, patt 21 sts, turn.
Row 18: Patt 22 sts, turn.
Row 19: Skpo, patt 66 sts, turn.
Rows 20–21: As rows 1–2.
Rows 22–23: As row 3.
Row 24: Patt 6 sts, turn.

Row 25: Patt 4 sts, k2tog, turn.
Rows 26–27: Patt 7 sts, turn.
Rows 28–29: Patt 9 sts, turn.
Rows 30–31: Patt 10 sts, turn.
Row 32: Patt 13 sts, turn.
Row 33: Patt 11 sts, k2tog, turn.
Row 34: Patt 15 sts, turn.
Row 35: Patt 13 sts, k2tog, turn.
Row 36: Patt 22 sts, turn.
Row 37: Patt 20 sts, k2tog, turn.
Row 38: Patt 62 sts, turn.

Working on these 62 sts only (in rows), complete peak as follows:

Row 39 (RS): Skpo, patt to last 2 sts, k2tog. (60 sts)
Row 40: Patt to end.
Row 41: Skpo, patt to last 2 sts, k2tog.
Row 42: P2tog, patt to last 2 sts, p2tog tbl.
Rows 43–46: Rep Rows 41–42 twice. (48 sts)
Row 47: Sl1, k2tog, psso, patt to last 3 sts, k3tog.
Row 48: P3tog, patt to last 3 sts, p3tog tbl.
Rows 49–54: Rep Rows 47–48 three times.

Cast (bind) off rem 16 sts.

PEAK LINING

Using 6.50mm (US 10½) needles and A, cast on 72 sts.

Row 1 (WS): Sl1, *p1, take yarn to back (RS) of work, slip next st purlwise, bring yarn to front (WS) of work; rep from * to end.

This row sets position of patt as given for Crown Panels.
Complete as given for Shape Peak from ** to end.

PEAK TRIM

Using 6.50mm (US 10½) dpns and B, cast on 3 sts.

Row 1: K3, *without turning work slip these 3 sts to opposite end of needle and bring yarn to opposite end of work, pulling it quite tightly across WS of work, now knit these 3 sts again; rep from * until Trim measures 29cm (11½in).
Cast (bind) off.

BUTTON COVER

Using 6.50mm (US 10½) needles and A, cast on 2 sts.

Row 1 (RS): Inc once in each st. (4 sts)
Row 2: Inc in first st, p2, inc in last st. (6 sts)
Row 3: Inc in first st, [k1, bring yarn to front (RS) of work, slip next st purlwise, take yarn to back (WS) of work] twice, inc in last st. (8 sts)
Row 4: [P1, take yarn to back (RS) of work, slip next st purlwise, bring yarn to front (WS) of work] four times.
Row 5: [K1, bring yarn to front (RS) of work, slip next st purlwise, take yarn to back (WS) of work] four times.
Row 6: As row 4.

Row 7: Skpo, [k1, bring yarn to front (RS) of work, slip next st purlwise, take yarn to back (WS) of work] twice, k2tog. (6 sts)
Row 8: P2tog, take yarn to back (RS) of work, slip next st purlwise, bring yarn to front (WS) of work, p1, p2tog tbl. (4 sts)
Row 9: Skpo, k2tog (2 sts).
Row 10: P2tog and fasten off.

FINISHING

Sew in all loose ends, then block and press the pieces.
Trim buckram to same size as Peak Lining section and tack (baste) in place to WS of Peak Lining. Matching edges of Peak and Peak Lining, pin and tack (baste) Peak Lining in place, sandwiching buckram between knitted layers. Using 3.75mm (F/5) crochet hook and A, work a round of dc (sc) around lower edge of Band and Peak, working sts around edge of Peak through Peak Lining as well (to join sections) and ending with ss (sl st) to first dc (sc). Fasten off. Slip stitch cast-on edge of Peak Lining in place on inside.
Sew Peak Trim around Band along top edge of Peak.
Following manufacturer's instructions, cover button with Button Cover, then attach to top of Cap.
Trim ribbon to fit neatly around inside of Band, allowing extra for seam. Join ends, then neatly slip stitch ribbon in place to inside of Band.

CROWNING GLORY

Before you sew the crown panels together, lay them out on a work surface and arrange them in a circle to best advantage. If you particularly like the stripe sequence on one panel, put that one at the front of the cap.
Sew together the row-ends of the crown panels using mattress stitch. To match the edges of the panels perfectly, lay one panel next to another and put a safety pin through both of the fasten-off points. Put another safety pin through the row-end edge of both pieces at the widest point of the section and a third pin through the row-end edges at the bottom, cast-on edge. Start sewing from the bottom edge.
Sew three pairs of panels together in this way. Then pin the three sections together in the same way and sew those seams.

DESIGNED BY

Rib Beanie

Chunky yarn, easy stripes and simple stitches mean that this is a great hat project for a novice knitter. When using the doubled yarn, just use one end from the outside and one end from the inside of the ball and treat them as though they were a single strand.

YARN

Rowan Cocoon (80% merino wool, 20% kid mohair), approx. 100g (3½oz)/115m (125yd) per ball

    One ball of Mountain 805 **(A)**
    One ball of Shale 804 **(C)**
    One ball of Alpine 802 **(E)**

Rowan Little Big Wool (67% wool, 33% nylon), approx. 50g (1¾oz)/60m (65yd) per ball

    One ball of Agate 511 **(B)**
    One ball of Topaz 509 **(D)**

NEEDLES

Pair of 8.00mm (US 11) knitting needles

EXTRAS

Tapestry needle

TENSION (GAUGE)

13 sts and 20 rows = 10cm (4in) square measured over St st using 8.00mm (US 11) needles.

TO FIT

One size

SKILL LEVEL

Beginner

SPECIAL NOTE

Use Rowan Cocoon DOUBLE throughout.

HAT

With A, cast on 62 sts.

Row 1 (RS): K2, [p2, k2] to end.
Row 2: P2, [k2, p2] to end.
These 2 rows form rib.
Keeping rib correct and cutting off and joining in colours as required, now work in stripes as follows:
Rows 3–4: With B.
Rows 5–6: With C.
Rows 7–8: With D.
Rows 9–10: With E.
Rows 11–12: With B.
Rows 13–16: With A.
Rows 17–18: With D.
Rows 19–20: With C.

SHAPE CROWN

Row 21: With C, *[k2, p2] twice, k2, p2tog; rep from * to last 2 sts, k2. (57 sts)
Row 22: With C, p2, *k1, p2, [k2, p2] twice; rep from * to end.
Row 23: With B, *[k2, p2] twice, k2, p1; rep from * to last 2 sts, k2.
Row 24: With B, p2, *k1, p2, [k2, p2] twice; rep from * to end.
Row 25: With E, *[k2, p2] twice, k1, k2tog; rep from * to last 2 sts, k2. (52 sts)
Row 26: With E, *[p4, k2, p2, k2], rep from * to last 2 sts, p2.
Row 27: With E, [k2, p2] twice, *k4, p2, k2, p2; rep from * to last 4 sts, k4.
Row 28: As row 26.

Row 29: With D, *[k2, p2] twice, k2tog; rep from * to last 2 sts, k2. (47 sts)
Row 30: With D, p3, [k2, p2, k2, p3] to last 8 sts, [k2, p2] twice.
Row 31: With A, k2, [p2, k2, p1, k3tog, k1] to end. (37 sts)
Row 32: With A, p2, [k1, p2, k2, p2] to end.
Row 33: With A, k2, [p2, k1, k3tog, k1] to end. (27 sts)
Row 34: With A, [p3, k2] to last 2 sts, p2.
Row 35: With A, k2, [p1, k3tog, k1] to end. (17 sts)
Row 36: With A, p2, [k1, p2] to end.
Cut off yarn and thread through rem 17 sts. Pull up tight and fasten off securely.

FINISHING

Sew in all loose ends. Do NOT press. Sew back seam using mattress stitch (see page 255), taking care to match up stripes.

BLANK CANVAS

This basic hat pattern can easily be customised without affecting the size or shape. You can knit it in a stripe sequence of your own invention, or in a plain colour with maybe just a stripe or two around the bottom edge as a border.

DESIGNED BY

Fiona McTague

LOVE THIS? Try knitting the Inca Satchel by Fiona on page 216.

Inca Hat

A palette of muted but clean and graphic colours takes away any hint of 'earth mother' that can otherwise creep into this style of hat, and the perky pompoms add a great finishing touch.

YARN

Rowan Baby Alpaca DK (100% baby alpaca), approx. 50g (1¾oz)/100m (109yd) per ball

Two balls of Jacob 205 **(A)**
One ball of Southdown 208 **(B)**
One ball of Lincoln 209 **(C)**

NEEDLES

Pair of 3.25mm (US 3) knitting needles
Pair of 3.75mm (US 5) knitting needles
One 3.25mm (US 3) circular knitting needle

EXTRAS

Stitch holder
Piece of stiff paper/cardboard for pompoms
Tapestry needle

TENSION (GAUGE)

24 sts and 36 rows = 10cm (4in) square measured over patt using 3.75mm (US 5) needles.

TO FIT

One size

SKILL LEVEL

Advanced

EARFLAPS (MAKE 2)

Using 3.75mm (US 5) needles and A, cast on 9 sts.

Row 1 (WS): Purl.

Starting with a knit row, cutting off and joining in yarns as required and stranding yarn not in use loosely across WS of work, now work in St st from chart A as follows:

Inc 1 st at each end of next 5 rows, then on foll 5 alt rows, taking inc sts into patt. (29 sts)

Cont straight until all 28 rows of Chart A have been completed, ending with a WS row.

Cut off yarn and leave sts on a holder.

MAIN SECTION

Using 3.75mm (US 5) needles and A, cast on 15 sts, turn and, with RS facing, knit across 29 sts of first Earflap, turn and cast on 33 sts, turn and, with RS facing, knit across 29 sts of second Earflap, turn and cast on 15 sts. (121 sts)

Join in C.

Row 1 (WS): With A p1, [with C p1, with A p1] to end.

Row 2: With C k1, [with A k1, with C k1] to end.

Row 3: With A, purl.

Repeating the 20-st patt rep six times across each row and working edge st as indicated, work in St st from Chart B until all 20 rows have been completed, ending with a WS row.

Row 24 (RS): With A, knit.

Row 25: With A, purl.

Row 26: With B, knit.

Row 27: As Row 25.

Row 28: As Row 2.

Row 29: As Row 1.

Row 30: As Row 24.

Row 31: With B, purl.

Row 32: As Row 24.

Row 33: With C p1, [with A p3, with C p1] to end.

Row 34: With B k2, [with A k1, with B k3] to last 3 sts, with A k1, with B k2.

Row 35: As Row 31.

SHAPE CROWN

Row 1 (RS): With A, [k10, k2tog] ten times, k1. (111 sts)

Row 2: With B, purl.

Row 3: With A, knit.

Row 4: With C p1, [with A p1, with C p1] to end.

Row 5: With A k1, [with C k1, with A k1] to end.

Row 6: With A, p1, [p2tog, p9] ten times. (101 sts)

Row 7: With B, knit.

Row 8: With A, p1, [p2tog, p8] ten times. (91 sts)

Row 9: With C, knit.

Row 10: With A, p1, [p2tog, p7] ten times. (81 sts)

Row 11: With B, knit.

Row 12: With A, p1, [p2tog, p6] ten times. (71 sts)

Row 13: As Row 5.

Row 14: As Row 4.

Row 15: With A, knit.

Row 16: With B, purl.

Row 17: With A, [k5, k2tog] ten times, k1. (61 sts)

Row 18: With C, purl.

Row 19: With A, [k4, k2tog] ten times, k1. (51 sts)

Row 20: With B, purl.

Row 21: With A, [k3, k2tog] ten times, k1. (41 sts)

Rows 22–23: As rows 4–5.

Row 24: With A, purl.

Row 25: With B, [k2, k2tog] ten times, k1. (31 sts)

Row 26: With A, purl.

Row 27: With C, [k1, k2tog] ten times, k1. (21 sts)

Row 28: With A, purl.

Row 29: With B, [k2tog] ten times, k1. Cut off yarn and thread through rem 11 sts. Pull up tight and fasten off securely.

LOWER BORDER

Using 3.25mm (US 3) circular needle and A, with RS facing pick up and knit across 15 sts from first cast-on edge of Main Section, 28 sts down row-end edge of first Earflap, 8 sts from cast-on edge of this Earflap, 28 sts up other row-end edge of this Earflap, 33 sts from next cast-on edge of Main Section, 28 sts down row-end edge of other Earflap, 8 sts from cast-on edge of this Earflap, 28 sts up other row-end edge

MAKE A STATEMENT

You could also knit this hat in a bright colour palette. Consider a strong aqua background with the Fair Isle worked in hot pink and tangerine, or a lime green background with turquoise and sea-blue patterning. Make the pompoms in either the background colour, as here, or make the cords in one of the Fair Isle colours and the pompoms in the other.

If you prefer, you can Swiss darn the reindeers' antlers after you have finished the knitting. Many knitters find it tricky to work single stitches neatly in intarsia and Swiss darning them is a good alternative.

of this Earflap, then 15 sts from rem cast-on edge of Main Section. (191 sts) Work 4 rows in garter st, ending with a RS row.
Cast (bind) off knitwise (on WS).

FINISHING

Sew in all loose ends, then block and press. Join back seam. With A, make two 5cm (2in) diameter pompoms (see page 36) and two twisted cords, each 13cm (5in) long. Attach a pompom to one end of one cord, then attach other end of cord to lower edge of Earflap as in photograph. Attach other cord and pompom to other Earflap in same way.

Chart A

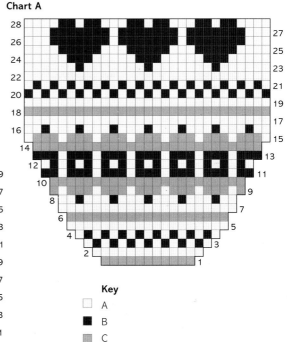

Chart B

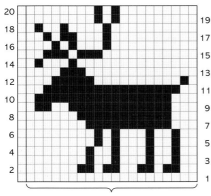

Key

☐ A

■ B

▨ C

LOVE THIS? Try knitting the Fair Isle Book Bag by Sue on page 192.

DESIGNED BY

Fair Isle Hat

Slouchy and easy to wear, this hat will look good if you have long or short hair, wayward curls or a sleek crop. Wear it pulled down, as here, or push it back on your forehead and let your fringe peep out.

YARN

Rowan Scottish Tweed 4-ply (100% wool), approx. 25g (1oz)/110m (120yd) per ball

Four balls of Oatmeal 025 **(A)**
One ball of Sea Green 006 **(B)**
One ball of Porridge 024 **(C)**
One ball of Peat 019 **(D)**
One ball of Rust 009 **(E)**
One ball of Gold 028 **(F)**

NEEDLES

Set of four 3.00mm (US 2) double-pointed needles (dpns)
Set of four 3.25mm (US 3) double-pointed needles (dpns)

EXTRAS

Tapestry needle

TENSION (GAUGE)

28 sts and 38 rows = 10cm (4in) square measured over St st using 3.25mm (US 3) needles.

TO FIT

One size

SKILL LEVEL

Intermediate

HAT

Using 3.00mm (US 2) needles and A, cast on 120 sts. Divide sts evenly across three dpns; join for working in the round.

Round 1: With A, [k2, p2] to end.
Round 2: As Round 1.
Join in E.
Round 3: With E, [k2, p2] to end.
Cut off E.
Rounds 4–9: As Round 1.
Change to 3.25mm (US 3) needles.
Round 10: With A, [rib 1, inc in next st] to end. (180 sts)
Rounds 11–12: Knit.
Repeating the 12-st patt rep 15 times around each round, work the 22 chart rows twice.
Cut off contrast yarn and cont using A only.
Rounds 57–58: Knit.

SHAPE CROWN

Round 59: [K2, k2tog] to end. (135 sts)
Round 60: Knit.
Round 61: [K25, k2tog] five times. (130 sts)
Round 62: [K24, k2tog] five times. (125 sts)
Round 63: [K23, k2tog] five times. (120 sts)
Round 64: [K22, k2tog] five times. (115 sts)
Round 65: [K21, k2tog] five times. (110 sts)
Round 66: [K20, k2tog] five times. (105 sts)
Cont in this way, working one fewer st between decreases on each round, until the foll round has been worked:
Round 79: [K7, k2tog] five times. (40 sts)

Round 80: [K2tog] twenty times.
Cut off yarn and thread through rem 20 sts. Pull tight and fasten off securely.

FINISHING

Sew in all loose ends, then block and press. With one strand of each colour, make a twisted cord approx. 14cm (5½ in) long and knot one end to form a short tassel. Attach other end of cord to top of Hat as in photograph.

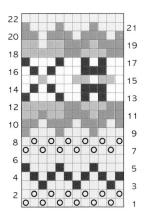

Key

 A (K on RS)
 A (P on RS)
B
C
D
E
F

DESIGNED BY

Beaded Beret

Beading brings instant glamour to knitting, as you can see from this fabulous beret. This isn't a remotely difficult technique to master – if you can knit, then you can bead knit – so choose your beads and get going.

YARN

Rowan 4-ply Soft (100% merino wool), approx.
50g (1¾oz)/175m (191yd) per ball
   Two balls of Tea Rose 401

NEEDLES

Set of four 3.25mm (US 3) double-pointed needles (dpns)

EXTRAS

Approx. 750 x 4mm clear glass beads
Sewing needle and thread
Six stitch markers
Length of 7mm (¼ in) wide elastic to fit around head
Tapestry needle

TENSION (GAUGE)

28 sts and 36 rows = 10cm (4in) square measured over St st using 3.25mm (US 3) needles.

TO FIT

One size

SKILL LEVEL

Intermediate

SPECIAL ABBREVIATIONS

See page 254 for information on B1.

BEADING NOTE

Before starting, thread beads onto yarn. To do this, thread a fine sewing needle (one that will easily pass through the beads) with sewing thread. Knot ends of thread and then pass end of yarn through this loop. Thread a bead onto the sewing thread, then slide it along and onto the knitting yarn. Continue in this way until the required number of beads are on the yarn.

MAIN SECTION

Cast on 156 sts. Divide sts evenly across three dpns; join for working in the round.

Round 1: [K26, PM] six times.

Round 2: *K1, B1, m1, [k3, m1] seven times, B1, k1, B1, SM to RH needle; rep from * five times. (204 sts)

Round 3: [K12, B1, k1, B1, k3, B1, k1, B1, k13, SM to RH needle] six times.

Round 4: [K11, B1, k3, B1, k1, B1, k3, B1, k11, B1, SM to RH needle] six times.

Round 5: [K16, B1, k17, SM to RH needle] six times.

Round 6: [K11, B1, k9, B1, k12, SM to RH needle] six times.

Round 7: [K7, m1, k5, B1, k7, B1, k5, m1, k8, SM to RH needle] six times. (216 sts)

Round 8: [K8, B1, k1, B1, k3, B1, k5, B1, k3, B1, k1, B1, k9, SM to RH needle] six times.

Round 9: *K7, [B1, k3] five times, B1, k8, SM to RH needle; rep from * five times.

Round 10: [K12, B1, k3, B1, k1, B1, k3, B1, k13, SM to RH needle] six times.

Round 11: *K7, B1, k5, [B1, k3] twice, B1, k5, B1, k8, SM to RH needle; rep from * five times.

Round 12: *K7, m1, k1, [B1, k5] three times, B1, k1, m1, k8, SM to RH needle; rep from * five times. (228 sts)

Round 13: [K10, B1, k5, B1, k3, B1, k5, B1, k11, SM to RH needle] six times.

Round 14: *K9, [B1, k5] three times, B1, k10, SM to RH needle; rep from * five times.

Round 15: [K8, B1, k5, B1, k3, B1, k3, B1, k5, B1, k9, SM to RH needle] six times.

Round 16: [K13, B1, k3, B1, k1, B1, k3, B1, k14, SM to RH needle] six times.

Round 17: *K7, m1, k1, [B1, k3] five times, B1, k1, m1, k8, SM to RH needle; rep from * five times. (240 sts)

Round 18: [K10, B1, k1, B1, k3, B1, k5, B1, k3, B1, k1, B1, k11, SM to RH needle] six times.

Round 19: [K15, B1, k7, B1, k16, SM to RH needle] six times.

Round 20: [K14, B1, k9, B1, k15, SM to RH needle] six times.

Round 21: [K19, B1, k20, SM to RH needle] six times.

Round 22: [K7, m1, k7, B1, k3, B1, k1, B1, k3, B1, k7, m1, k8, SM to RH needle] six times. (252 sts)

Round 23: [K16, B1, k1, B1, k3, B1, k1, B1, k17, SM to RH needle] six times.

Round 24: [K36, wrap next st (by slipping next st from LH needle to RH needle, taking yarn to opposite side of work between needles and then slipping same st back onto LH needle – when working back across wrapped sts, work the wrapped st and the wrapping loop tog as one st) and turn, p31, wrap next st and turn, k21, wrap next st and turn, p11, wrap next st and turn, k16, wrap next st and turn, p21, wrap next st and turn, k29, wrap next st and turn, p37, wrap next st and turn, k40, SM to RH needle] six times.

Round 25: Knit.

Round 26: [Skpo, k37, k2tog, k1, SM to RH needle] six times. (240 sts)
Rounds 27–28: Knit.
Round 29: [Skpo, k17, B1, k17, k2tog, k1, SM to RH needle] six times. (228 sts)
Round 30: Knit.
Round 31: [K18, B1, k19] six times.
Round 32: [Skpo, k33, k2tog, k1, SM to RH needle] six times. (216 sts)
Round 33: [K17, B1, k18] six times.
Round 34: Knit.
Round 35: *Skpo, k13, [B1, k1] twice, B1, k13, k2tog, k1, SM to RH needle; rep from * five times. (204 sts)
Round 36: Knit.
Round 37: *K12, [B1, k3] twice, B1, k13, SM to RH needle; rep from * five times.
Round 38: [Skpo, k29, k2tog, k1, SM to RH needle] six times. (192 sts)
Round 39: *K9, [B1, k5] twice, B1, k10, SM to RH needle; rep from * five times.
Round 40: Knit.
Round 41: *Skpo, k5, [B1, k7] twice, B1, k5, k2tog, k1, SM to RH needle; rep from * five times. (180 sts)
Round 42: Knit.

Round 43: *K12, [B1, k1] twice, B1, k13, SM to RH needle; rep from * five times .
Round 44: [Skpo, k25, k2tog, k1, SM to RH needle] six times. (168 sts)
Round 45: *K9, [B1, k3] twice, B1, k10, SM to RH needle; rep from * five times.
Round 46: Knit.
Round 47: *Skpo, k5, [B1, k5] three times, k2tog, k1, SM to RH needle; rep from * five times. (156 sts)
Round 48: Knit.
Round 49: [K12, B1, k13, SM to RH needle] six times.
Round 50: [Skpo, k21, k2tog, k1, SM to RH needle] six times. (144 sts)
Round 51: *K9, [B1, k1] twice, B1, k10, SM to RH needle; rep from * five times.
Round 52: Knit.
Round 53: *Skpo, k5, [B1, k3] twice, B1, k5, k2tog, k1, SM to RH needle; rep from * five times. (132 sts)
Round 54: Knit.
Round 55: [K10, B1, k11, SM to RH needle] six times.

Round 56: [Skpo, k17, k2tog, k1, SM to RH needle] six times. (120 sts)
Round 57: [K9, B1, k10, SM to RH needle] six times.
Round 58: Knit.
Round 59: *Skpo, k5, [B1, k1] twice, B1, k5, k2tog, k1, SM to RH needle; rep from * five times. (108 sts)
Round 60: Knit.
Round 61: [K8, B1, k9, SM to RH needle] six times.
Round 62: [Skpo, k13, k2tog, k1, SM to RH needle] six times. (96 sts)
Round 63: [K7, B1, k8, SM to RH needle] six times.
Round 64: [Skpo, k11, k2tog, k1, SM to RH needle] six times. (84 sts)
Round 65: [K6, B1, k7, SM to RH needle] six times.
Round 66: [Skpo, k9, k2tog, k1, SM to RH needle] six times. (72 sts)
Round 67: Knit.
Round 68: [Skpo, k7, k2tog, k1, SM to RH needle] six times. (60 sts)
Round 69: Knit.
Round 70: [Skpo, k5, k2tog, k1, SM to RH needle] six times. (48 sts)
Round 71: Knit.

Round 72: [Skpo, k3, k2tog, k1,
SM to RH needle] six times. (36 sts)
Round 73: Knit.
Round 74: [Skpo, k1, k2tog, k1,
SM to RH needle] six times. (24 sts)
Round 75: Knit.
Round 76: [Sl1, k2tog, psso, k1,
remove M] six times.
Cut off yarn and thread through
rem 12 sts. Pull up tight and fasten
off securely.

BAND

With RS facing, pick up and knit 156 sts
around cast-on edge of Main Section.
Divide sts evenly across three dpns and
work in rounds as follows:
Round 1: Knit.
Rep this round until Band measures
4cm (1½ in) from pick-up round.
Cast (bind) off.

FINISHING

Sew in all loose ends, then block and
press fabric, taking great care not to
damage beads.
Join ends of elastic to form a ring. Fold
Band in half to inside and neatly sew
cast-off (bound-off) edge to pick-up
round, enclosing elastic in this casing.
Make a 7cm (2¾ in) long tassel and
separate strands of yarn within tassel.
Attach tassel to centre of crown.

SPARKLE MAGIC

If you want to use different beads
to those stated in the pattern, there
are a couple of simple rules to
follow. First, the hole in the beads
must be large enough to slip over
doubled yarn so that you can
thread the beads onto the yarn. It
doesn't matter if they are a tight fit
on doubled yarn as they only need
to travel over a short distance of
this before they slide onto the single
thickness of yarn.
Second, the beads must not be
larger than the knitted stitch or they
won't lie neat and flat against the
knitted fabric. Knit a tension (gauge)
swatch and take it with you to the
bead shop when buying your beads.
Lay one of your chosen beads on
the swatch and check it fits within a
stitch before buying.

DESIGNED BY

Paris Beret

As chic as the city it's named for, you can wear this beret with denims, with a fitted dress or with a slimline coat – anything with a sleek silhouette. The herringbone pattern border defines the shaping and adds understated texture.

YARN

Rowan Kid Classic (70% lambswool, 26% kid mohair, 4% nylon), approx. 50g (1¾oz)/140m (153yd) per ball
  One ball of Feather 828

NEEDLES

Pair of 3.75mm (US 5) knitting needles
Pair of 5.00mm (US 8) knitting needles

EXTRAS

Tapestry needle

TENSION (GAUGE)

18 sts and 25 rows = 10cm (4in) square measured over St st using 5.00mm (US 8) needles.

TO FIT

One size

SKILL LEVEL

Intermediate

HAT

Using 3.75mm (US 5) needles, cast on 111 sts.

Row 1 (RS): K1, [p1, k1] to end.
Row 2: P1, [k1, p1] to end.
These 2 rows form rib.
Cont in rib for 10 rows more, dec 1 st at end of last row and ending with a WS row. (110 sts)
Change to 5.00mm (US 8) needles.
Now work in herringbone patt as follows:
Row 13 (RS): K1, *sl1, k1, psso but leave this st on LH needle, now knit into back of this (slipped) st; rep from * to end.
Row 14: *P2tog leaving sts on LH needle, then purl first of these 2 sts again and slip both sts off LH needle; rep from * to end.
These 2 rows form herringbone patt.
Work in the herringbone patt for 6 rows more.
Row 21 (RS): K1, m1, knit to end. (111 sts)
Row 22: Purl.
Row 23: [K10, m1] eleven times, k1. (122 sts)
Row 24: Purl.
Row 25: Knit.
Row 26: Purl.
Row 27: [K11, m1] eleven times, k1. (133 sts)

Rows 28–29: As Rows 24–25.
Row 30: Purl to last st, pfb. (134 sts)
Rows 31–32: As Rows 13–14.

SHAPE CROWN

Row 33: K1, [k10, skpo] eleven times, k1. (123 sts)
Row 34 and every foll alt row: Purl.
Row 35: Knit.
Row 37: K1, [k9, skpo] eleven times, k1. (112 sts)
Row 39: Knit.
Row 41: K1, [k8, skpo] eleven times, k1. (101 sts)
Row 43: Knit.
Row 45: K1, [k7, skpo] eleven times, k1. (90 sts)
Row 47: K1, [k6, skpo] eleven times, k1. (79 sts)
Row 49: K1, [k5, skpo] eleven times, k1. (68 sts)
Row 51: K1, [k4, skpo] eleven times, k1. (57 sts)
Row 53: K1, [k3, skpo] eleven times, k1. (46 sts)
Row 55: K1, [k2, skpo] eleven times, k1. (35 sts)
Row 57: K1, [k1, skpo] eleven times, k1. (24 sts)
Row 58: Purl.
Cut off yarn and thread through rem 24 sts. Pull up tight and fasten off securely.

FINISHING

Sew in all loose ends, then block and press. Sew back seam using mattress stitch (see page 255).

DESIGNED BY

Rose Cap

This cap may look a bit complicated for a beginner, but it's actually just combinations of plain knit and purl stitches and the basic increases and decreases. So if you are a new knitter, don't be afraid to give this pattern a go.

YARN

Debbie Bliss Donegal Chunky Tweed (100% wool), approx. 100g (3½oz)/100m (109yd) per skein

    One skein of Peacock 09 **(A)**

Coats Anchor Tapisserie Wool (100% wool), approx. 10m (11yd) per skein

    Two skeins of red 8202 **(B)**

    One skein of burgundy 9274 **(C)**

NEEDLES

Pair of 4.50mm (US 7) knitting needles

Pair of 7.00mm (US 10½) knitting needles

EXTRAS

Tapestry needle

TENSION (GAUGE)

12 sts and 18 rows = 10cm (4in) square measured over St st using 7.00mm (US 10½) needles and A.

TO FIT

One size

SKILL LEVEL

Beginner

HAT

Using 7.00mm (US 10¹/₂) needles and
A, cast on 63 sts.
Row 1 (RS): K1, [p1, k1] to end.
Row 2: P1, [k1, p1] to end.
Rep rows 1–2 twice more.
Row 7 (RS): [P20, pfb] three times.
(66 sts)
**Row 8 and every foll alt row (to
row 20):** Knit.
Row 9: [Pfb, p10] six times. (72 sts)
Row 11: [Pfb, p11] six times. (78 sts)
Row 13: [Pfb, p12] six times. (84 sts)
Row 15: [Pfb, p13] six times. (90 sts)
Row 17: [Pfb, p14] six times. (96 sts)
Row 19: [Pfb, p15] six times. (102 sts)
Rows 20–21: Knit.
**Row 22 and every foll WS row to
end:** Purl.
Row 23: K1, [k3tog, k7] ten times, k1.
(82 sts)
Row 25: Knit.
Row 27: K1, [k3tog, k5] ten times, k1.
(62 sts)
Row 29: Knit.
Row 31: K1, [k3tog, k3] ten times, k1.
(42 sts)

Row 33: Knit.
Row 35: K1, [k3tog, k1] ten times, k1.
(22 sts)
Row 37: Knit.
Row 39: [K2tog] eleven times. (11 sts)
Row 40: Purl.
Cut off yarn and thread through
rem 11 sts. Pull up tight and fasten
off securely.

ROSE

Using 4.50mm (US 7) needles and B,
cast on 80 sts.
Starting with a knit row, work in St st for
9 rows, ending with a WS row.
Cast (bind) off, leaving a long tail.

LEAF

Using 4.50mm (US 7) needles and B,
cast on 5 sts.
Row 1 (RS): K1, [kfb, k1] twice. (7 sts)
Row 2: P7.
Row 3: K1, kfb, k3, kfb, k1. (9 sts)
Row 4: P9.
Row 5: K1, kfb, k5, kfb, k1. (11 sts)
Starting with a purl row, work in St st
for 5 rows, ending with a WS row.

Row 11 (RS): K1, k2tog, k5, skpo, k1.
(9 sts)
Row 12: P1, p2tog tbl, p3, p2tog, p1.
(7 sts)
Row 13: K1, k2tog, k1, skpo, k1.
(5 sts)
Row 14: P2tog tbl, p1, p2tog. (3 sts)
Row 15: K3tog and fasten off.

FINISHING

Sew in all loose ends, then block and
press pieces, steaming Rose and Leaf
quite hard to felt them slightly.
Sew back seam of Hat using mattress
stitch (see page 255). To form 'points',
lay Hat flat and pinch each 'point'
(where shaping occurs) and secure
layers together with a few stitches
on inside.
Roll up Rose strip to form a rose shape
and, using the long tail of yarn, secure
cast-off (bound-off) edges together at
base of Rose. Sew Rose to Hat as in
photograph, attaching Leaf next to it.

DESIGNED BY

Beaded Beanie

Fashionistas will adore this gothic beanie with its fluffy, beaded edging and oversize flower. Knit another flower the same and wear it as a corsage on your lapel or sew it to a ribbon and tie it around your wrist.

YARN

Rowan Felted Tweed DK (50% merino wool, 25% alpaca, 25% viscose), approx. 50g (1¾oz)/175m (191yd) per ball
   One ball of Carbon 159 **(A)**
Rowan Kidsilk Haze (70% super kid mohair, 30% silk), approx. 25g (1oz)/210m (229yd) per ball
   One ball of Wicked 599 **(B)**

NEEDLES

Pair of 3.00mm (US 3) knitting needles
Pair of 3.75mm (US 5) knitting needles

EXTRAS

Approx. 100 small black glass beads
Sewing needle and thread
Tapestry needle

TENSION

23 sts and 32 rows = 10cm (4in) square measured over St st using 3.75mm (US 5) needles and A.

TO FIT

One size

SKILL LEVEL

Intermediate

SPECIAL ABBREVIATIONS

See page 254 for information on B1.

BEADING NOTE

Before starting, thread beads onto B. To do this, thread a fine sewing needle (one that will easily pass through the beads) with sewing thread. Knot ends of thread and then pass end of yarn through this loop. Thread a bead onto the sewing thread, then slide it along and onto the knitting yarn. Continue in this way until the required number of beads are on the yarn.

HAT

Thread approx. 90 beads onto B.
Using 3.00mm (US 3) needles and
two strands of B held together, cast
on 119 sts.

Row 1 (RS): K1, [p1, B1, p1, k1] to
last 2 sts, p1, k1.

Row 2: P1, [k1, p1] to end.

Row 3: K1, [p1, k1, p1, B1] to last
2 sts, p1, k1.

Row 4: As Row 2.

Row 5: As Row 1.

Row 6: Pfb, k1, [p1, k1] to last st, pfb.
(121 sts)

Cut off B and join in A.
Change to 3.75mm (US 5) needles.
Starting with a knit row, work in St st
until Hat measures 10cm (4in), ending
with a WS row.

SHAPE CROWN

Row 1 (RS): [K10, k2tog] ten times, k1.
(111 sts)

Work 3 rows.

Row 5: [K9, k2tog] ten times, k1.
(101 sts)

Work 3 rows.

Row 9: [K8, k2tog] ten times, k1. (91 sts)

Work 1 row.

Row 11: [K7, k2tog] ten times, k1.
(81 sts)

Work 1 row.

Row 13: [K6, k2tog] ten times, k1.
(71 sts)

Work 1 row.

Row 15: [K5, k2tog] ten times, k1.
(61 sts)
Work 1 row.
Row 17: [K4, k2tog] ten times, k1.
(51 sts)
Work 1 row.
Row 19: [K3, k2tog] ten times, k1.
(41 sts)
Work 1 row.
Row 21: [K2, k2tog] ten times, k1.
(31 sts)
Work 1 row.
Row 23: [K1, k2tog] ten times, k1.
(21 sts)
Work 1 row.
Row 25: [K2tog] ten times, k1.
Cut off yarn and thread through
rem 11 sts. Pull up tight and fasten
off securely.

FLOWER PETALS

Using 3.00mm (US 3) needles and two
strands of B held together, cast on 9 sts.
Row 1 (RS): K1, [p1, k1] to end.
**Row 2: As Row 1.
These 2 rows form moss (seed) st.
Keeping moss (seed) st correct, cont as
follows:
Row 3: K1, m1, moss (seed) st to end.
(10 sts)
Work 1 row.
Rep last 2 rows. (11 sts)
Work 2 rows.
Row 9: K2tog tbl, moss (seed) st to
end. (10 sts)
Work 1 row.

Rep last 2 rows. (9 sts)
Cast (bind) off 4 sts at beg of next row.
(5 sts)
Work 1 row.***
Cast on 4 sts at beg of next row.
(9 sts)****
Rep from ** to **** four times more, then
from ** to *** again.
Cast (bind) off rem 5 sts.

FLOWER CENTRE

Using 3.00mm (US 3) needles and A,
cast on 3 sts.
Row 1 (RS): K3.
Row 2 and every foll alt row: Purl.
Row 3: K1, [m1, k1] twice. (5 sts)
Row 5: K1, m1, k3, m1, k1. (7 sts)
Row 7: K2tog, k3, k2tog. (5 sts)
Row 9: K2tog, k1, k2tog. (3 sts)
Row 10: P3.
Cast (bind) off.

FINISHING

Sew in all loose ends, then block and
press the pieces, taking care not to
damage the beads.
Sew up back seam of Hat using
mattress stitch (see page 255).
Join cast-on and cast-off (bound-off)
ends of Flower Petals. Run gathering
threads around straight row-end edge
and pull up to form flower. Sew Flower
Centre in place at centre of Flower
Petals. Sew completed flower to Hat as
in photograph, attaching rem beads to
Flower Centre.

BROOCH THE SUBJECT

Customise this hat design by
swapping the flower for a brooch
and choosing beads in a colour to
match it. Don't choose a very heavy
brooch or it will pull the knitted
fabric out of shape.

DESIGNED BY

Lattice Beanie

Knitted with three ends of yarn on big, straight needles, this little hat will knit up in a flash. The subtle colour changes, which are created by using two different yarn colours together, complement the textured stitch pattern beautifully.

YARN

Rowan Cocoon (80% merino wool, 20% kid mohair), approx. 100g (3½oz)/ 115m (125yd) per ball
 Two balls of Scree 803 **(A)**
 One ball of Alpine 802 **(B)**

NEEDLES

Pair of 10.00mm (US 15) knitting needles

EXTRAS

Tapestry needle

TENSION (GAUGE)

9 sts and 12 rows = 10cm (4in) square measured over St st using 10.00mm (US 15) needles and 2 strands of A and 1 strand of B held together.

TO FIT

One size

SKILL LEVEL

Intermediate

HAT

With two strands of A and one strand of B held together (three strands in total), cast on 41 sts.

Row 1 (RS): K1, [p1, k1] to end.

Row 2: P1, [k1, p1] to end.

Row 3: *P1, k1, yfwd, skpo, p1, k1, p1, k2, p1, m1; rep from * to last st, k1. (45 sts)

Row 4: K1, *k2, [p1, k1] twice, p2tog tbl, yrn, p2, k1; rep from * to end.

Row 5: *[P1, k1] twice, yfwd, skpo, p1, k2, p2, m1; rep from * to last st, p1. (49 sts)

Row 6: K1, *k3, p1, k1, p2tog tbl, yrn, p1, k1, p2, k1; rep from * to end.

Row 7: *[P1, k1] three times, yfwd, skpo, k1, p3, m1; rep from * to last st, p1. (53 sts)

Row 8: K1, *k4, p2tog tbl, yrn, [p1, k1] twice, p2, k1; rep from * to end.

Row 9: *P1, k1, yfwd, skpo, p1, k1, p1, k2, p4; rep from * to last st, p1.

Row 10: K1, *k4, [p1, k1] twice, p2tog tbl, yrn, p2, k1; rep from * to end.

Row 11: *[P1, k1] twice, yfwd, skpo, p1, k2, p4; rep from * to last st, p1.

Row 12: K1, *k4, p1, k1, p2tog tbl, yrn, p1, k1, p2, k1; rep from * to end.

Row 13: *[P1, k1] three times, yfwd, skpo, k1, p4; rep from * to last st, p1.

Row 14: K1, *k4, p2tog tbl, yrn, [p1, k1] twice, p2, k1; rep from * to end.

Rows 15–18: As rows 9–12.

Row 19: *[P1, k1] three times, yfwd, skpo, k1, p2, p2tog; rep from * to last st, p1. (49 sts)

Row 20: K1, *k3, p2tog tbl, yrn, [p1, k1] twice, p2, k1; rep from * to end.

Row 21: *P1, k1, yfwd, skpo, p1, k1, p1, k2, p1, p2tog; rep from * to last st, p1. (45 sts)

Row 22: K1, *k2, [p1, k1] twice, p2tog tbl, yrn, p2, k1; rep from * to end.

Row 23: *[P1, k1] twice, yfwd, skpo, p1, k2, p2tog; rep from * to last st, p1. (41 sts)

Row 24: *K2tog, p1, k1, p2tog tbl, yrn, p1, k1, p2; rep from * to last st, k1. (37 sts)

Row 25: *K2tog, [p1, k1] twice, yfwd, skpo, k1; rep from * to last st, p1. (33 sts)

Row 26: K1, *p2tog tbl, yrn, [p1, k1] twice, p2; rep from * to end.

Row 27: *[K1, p1] twice, k1, k3tog; rep from * to last st, k1. (25 sts)

Row 28: P1, *p3tog, k1, p1, k1; rep from * to end.

Cut off yarn and thread through rem 17 sts. Pull up tight and fasten off securely.

FINISHING

Sew in all loose ends. Do NOT press. Sew back seam using mattress stitch (see page 255).

IN TRIPLE TIME

If you find the three ends of yarn tricky to handle, you can wind up one big ball made up of all three yarns before you start the knitting.

Socks

Never have cold toes again! Whether you're lounging on the settee or making an eye-catching statement, one of these designs is for you. Pull out your double-pointed needles and get to work with the simple and cute I ♥ Socks pattern or challenge yourself to some lace work with the Vandyke Lace Socks. Remember to pull firmly on the yarn as you move between needles to avoid ladders!

DESIGNED BY

Striper Socks

These snazzy socks use so little of each colour that many pairs can be made with the quantities given. Try changing the colours around to give you a completely different pair of socks using the same pattern.

YARN

Rowan Wool Cotton (50% merino wool, 50% cotton), approx. 50g (1¾oz)/113m (124yd) per ball

One ball of Flower 943 **(A)**
One ball of Elf 946 **(B)**
One ball of Inky 908 **(C)**
One ball of Antique 900 **(D)**
One ball of Poster Blue 948 **(E)**
One ball of Pumpkin 962 **(F)**
One ball of Gypsy 910 **(G)**
One ball of Citron 901 **(H)**
One ball of Rich 911 **(I)**
One ball of Aloof 958 **(J)**

NEEDLES

Set of four 3.50mm (US 4) double-pointed needles (dpns)

EXTRAS

Three stitch markers
Tapestry needle

TENSION (GAUGE)

24 sts and 32 rows = 10cm (4in) square measured over St st using 3.50mm (US 4) needles.

TO FIT

One size

SKILL LEVEL

Intermediate

SOCKS (MAKE 2)

Using A and Continental method, cast on 48 sts. Divide sts evenly across three dpns; join for working in the round.

Rounds 1–6: Work in k1, p1 rib.

Round 7: Knit.

Cut off A, join in B.

Rounds 8–10: Knit.

Cut off B. Using Fair Isle technique, work as follows:

Rounds 11–13: [K2 with C, k2 with D]; rep to end of round.

Rounds 14–16: [K2 with D, k2 with C]; rep to end of round. Cut off C and D.

Rounds 17–19· K with B. Cut off B.

Rounds 20–21: K with E. Cut off E.

Rounds 22–23: K with F. Cut off F.

Rounds 24–25: K with G. Cut off G.

Rounds 26–27: K with H. Cut off H.

Rounds 28–29: K with I. Cut off I.

Rounds 30–31: K with J. Cut off J.

Round 32: K with A.

Round 33: K12, PM, k24, PM, k12. Cut off A.

HEEL FLAP

Rearrange sts for knitting heel flap by placing 24 sts between markers on one needle (to be worked later). Place 12 sts before first marker and 12 sts after second marker, on one needle, to be knitted back and forth for heel flap.

Row 1: [K1, sl1] with A to end of row.

Row 2: Purl.

Rep last 2 rows until Heel Flap measures 6.25cm (2½in).

TURN HEEL

Next row: K12, PM, k12.

Next row: P to M, SM, p2, p2tog, p1, turn.

Next row: K to M, SM, k2, k2tog, k1, turn.

Remove M in next row.

Next row: P7, p2tog, p1, turn.

Next row: K8, k2tog, k1, turn.

Next row: P9, p2tog, p1, turn.

Next row: K10, k2tog, k1, turn.

Next row: P11, p2tog, p1, turn.

Next row: K12, k2tog, k1, turn.

Next row: P13, p2tog, turn.

Next row: K13, k2tog. (14 sts on heel) Cut off A.

FOOT

Round 1: With D, pick up and knit 12 sts along right side of heel flap, k7 of heel sts (N1), k7 rem heel sts, pick up and knit 12 sts along left side of Heel Flap (N2), k24 on holding needle (N3).

Round 2: With C, ssk, knit to last 2 sts on N1, k2tog, knit to end of round.

Round 3: Knit with D.

Rep last 2 rounds until 48 sts rem.

Next round: Knit with C.

Next round: Knit with D.

Rep last 2 rounds until foot measures 16.25cm (6½in) from back of heel, or 5cm (2in) shorter than desired length of foot. Cut off C and D.

TOE

Round 1: K with A.

Round 2: K to last 3 sts of N3, ssk, k1.

Round 3: K1, k2tog, k to last 3 sts of N2, ssk, k2, k2tog, k to end of round.

Rep last 2 rounds until 32 sts rem.

Next round: K to last 3 sts of N3, ssk, k1.

Next round: K1, k2tog, k to last 3 sts of N2, ssk, k2, k2tog, k to last 3 sts of N3, ssk, k1.

Rep last round until 19 sts rem.

Next round: K1, k2tog, k to last 3 sts of N2, ssk, k2, k2tog, k to end of round. (16 sts)

FINISHING

Weave toe stitches together using Kitchener stitch (see page 256). Sew in all loose ends.

SWITCHBACK

- Throughout the pattern, take care when switching colours so as not to leave a hole in the fabric.
- For the stripe portion of the foot, it is not necessary to cut the yarn after every round. You can twist the old yarn with the new before the first stitch of each round.

DESIGNED BY

Stephanie Mrse

Skull Socks

Channel your bad girl nature with skull socks, knitted in the softest yarn, to please the edgiest fashion mavens.

YARN

Debbie Bliss Merino DK (100% merino wool), approx. 50g (1¾oz)/110m (120yd) per ball

- Three balls of Black 300 **(MC)**
- One ball of White 100 **(A)**

NEEDLES

Set of five 3.00mm (US 2) double-pointed needles (dpns)
Set of five 3.25mm (US 3) double-pointed needles (dpns)

EXTRAS

Two stitch markers
Tapestry needle

TENSION (GAUGE)

26 sts and 34 rows = 10cm (4in) square measured over St st using 3.25mm (US 3) needles.

TO FIT

One size

SKILL LEVEL

Advanced

SOCKS (MAKE 2)
LEG
Using 3.00mm (US 2) needles and MC, loosely cast on 64 sts using Continental method.

Divide sts evenly across four dpns, being careful not to twist stitches.

Work in k2, p2 rib for 4cm (1½in).

Change to 3.25mm (US 3) needles and knit 1 round, PM after first 4 sts and before last 4 sts.

Knit chart Rows 1–16 once.

Knit chart Rows 1–12 once.

START DECREASE
Round 13a: K1, k2tog, knit to last 3 sts, ssk, k1.
Round 14a: Knit.
Round 15a: As Round 13a. (60 sts)
Round 16a: Knit.
Knit chart rows 1–12 once.
Round 13b: K2tog, knit to last 2 sts, ssk.
Round 14b: Knit.
Round 15b: As Round 13b. (56 sts)
Round 16b: Knit.
Knit chart rows 1–16 once.
Round 17: K1, k2tog, knit to last 3 sts, ssk, k1.
Round 18: Knit.
Round 19: K1, k2tog, knit to last 3 sts, ssk, k1. (52 sts)
Round 20: Knit.
Round 21: K2tog, knit to last 2 sts, ssk.
Round 22: Knit.

Round 23: As Round 21 (48 sts).
Cont to knit straight until work measures 30cm (12in) from cast on, or desired length.

HEEL FLAP
Work over centre back 24 sts.
Row 1: [Sl1 knitwise, k1] twelve times.
Row 2: Sl1 purlwise, p23.
Rep Rows 1–2 until heel flap measures 6.5cm (2in), ending with a Row 2.

TURN HEEL
Next row: Sl1, k13, ssk, k1, turn.
Next row: Sl1, p5, p2tog, p1, turn.
Next row: Sl1, k6, ssk, k1, turn.
Next row: Sl1, p7, p2tog, p1, turn.
Cont in this way until all sts are worked. (14 sts)
Next row: K14.

GUSSETS
Pick up 14 sts along side of heel flap, k across 24 sts of instep, pick up 14 sts along other side of heel flap.
Divide heel sts between first and fourth needles (N1 and N4).
Round 1: Knit.
Round 2: N1 – k to last 3 sts, k2tog, k1; N2 – k12; N3 – k12; N4 – k1, ssk, k rem sts.
Rep Rounds 1–2 until 48 sts rem.

FOOT
Work straight until foot measures about 5cm (2in) shorter than desired length of sock.

TOE SHAPING
Round 1: N1 – k to last 3 sts, k2tog, k1; N2 – k1, ssk, k rem sts; N3 – k to last 3 sts, k2tog, k1; N4 – k1, ssk, k rem sts.
Round 2: Knit.
Rep Rounds 1–2 until 20 sts rem.
Cut yarn, leaving a 30cm (12in) tail for sewing in.

FINISHING
Weave toe together with Kitchener stitch (see page 256). Sew in all loose ends.

Key
☐ A
■ MC

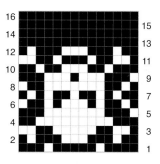

NEEDLE POINT

You might want to go up one needle size when working the chart, since Fair Isle tends to pull in the fabric and is less stretchy than regular stocking (stockinette) stitch.

DESIGNED BY

These cute ankle socks add a little heart and sole to footwear. For longer socks, knit the chart section twice or more.

YARN

Debbie Bliss Merino DK (100% merino wool), approx. 50g (1¾oz)/110m (120yd) per ball

    Two balls of White 100 **(MC)**

    One ball of Purple 608 **(A)**

    One ball of Red 700 **(B)**

NEEDLES

Set of five 3.25mm (US 3) double-pointed needles (dpns)

EXTRAS

Tapestry needle

TENSION (GAUGE)

26 sts and 34 rows = 10cm (4in) square measured over St st using 3.25mm (US 3) needles.

TO FIT

One size

SKILL LEVEL

Advanced

SOCKS (MAKE 2)

CUFF

Using MC, loosely cast on 48 sts using
Continental method.
Divide sts evenly across four dpns, being
careful not to twist sts.
Knit in k2, p2 rib for 4cm (1½ in).
Next round: Knit.
Knit heart and stripes chart once.
Knit 5 rows in MC.

HEEL FLAP

Work over 24 sts.
Row 1: [Sl1 knitwise, k1] twelve times.
Row 2: Sl1 purlwise, p23.
Rep Rows 1–2 until heel flap measures
6.5cm (2½in), ending with a Row 2.

TURN HEEL

Next row: Sl1, k13, ssk, k1, turn.
Next row: Sl1, p5, p2tog, p1, turn.
Next row: Sl1, k6, ssk, k1, turn.
Next row: Sl1, p7, p2tog, p1, turn.
Cont in this way until all sts are worked.
(14 sts)
Next row: K7, change to A, k7.

GUSSETS

Pick up 14 sts along side of heel flap,
knit across 24 sts of instep, pick up
14 sts along other side of heel flap.
Divide heel sts between first and fourth
needles (N1 and N4).
Round 1: Knit.

Round 2: N1 – k to last 3 sts, k2tog,
k1; N2 – k12; N3 – k12; N4 – k1, ssk,
k rem sts.
Rep Rounds 1–2 until 48 sts rem.

FOOT

Work straight until foot measures about
5cm (2in) shorter than desired length
of sock.

SHAPE TOE

Round 1: N1 – k to last 3 sts, k2tog,
k1; N2 – k1, ssk, k rem sts; N3 –
k to last 3 sts, k2tog, k1; N4 – k1,
ssk, k rem sts.
Round 2: Knit.
Rep Rounds 1–2 until there are
20 sts rem.
Cut yarn, leaving a 30cm (12in) tail for
sewing in.

FINISHING

Weave toe together with Kitchener stitch
(see page 256). Sew in all loose ends.

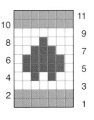

Key
- A
- MC
- B

SMOOTH OPERATOR

Be careful not to produce any hard
lumps or bumps – which would
chafe the foot – when sewing in
the ends.

DESIGNED BY

Gosia Dzik-Holden

Silk Hose

Pure silk gives a luxurious feel to these stockings and the bright, jewel-like colours create a great look.

YARN

Debbie Bliss Pure Silk (100% silk), approx. 50g (1¾oz)/ 125m (137yd) per ball

- Five balls of Aqua 07 **(MC)**
- Two balls of Coral 12 **(A)**

NEEDLES

Set of five 2.00mm (US 0) double-pointed needles (dpns)

EXTRAS

Stitch marker
Tapestry needle

TENSION (GAUGE)

14 sts and 19 rows = 5cm (2in) square measured over St st using 2.00mm (US 0) needles.

TO FIT

One size

SKILL LEVEL

Intermediate

STOCKINGS (MAKE 2)
LEG
Working with double yarn (1 strand of MC and 1 of A), cast on 80 sts on one needle using Continental method. Divide sts evenly across four dpns and join for working in the round, being careful not to twist sts. Place marker after first st to denote beg of round. Cut off A, work to end with single strand of MC. Knit 1 round.

CUFF
Round 1: *K2, p2; rep from * to end of round.
Rep this round nineteen times more; work measures about 5cm (2in) from beg.

BEGIN FAGGOTED PATTERN
Multiple of 20 sts.
Rounds 1, 3, 5: *P4, [k1 tbl, k1] twice, [yo, p2tog] four times, [k1, k1 tbl] twice; rep from * to end.
Rounds 2, 4, 6: *P4, [k1 tbl, p1] twice, [k2tog, yo] four times, [p1, k1 tbl] twice; rep from * to end.
Rounds 7, 9, 11: *P4, k1 tbl, k1, k1 tbl, k10, k1 tbl, k1, k1 tbl; rep from * to end.

Rounds 8, 10, 12: *P4, [k1 tbl, p1] twice, k8, p1, k1 tbl, [p1, k1 tbl] twice; rep from * to end.
Rep Rounds 1–12 twice more and Rounds 1–6 once.
Round 31: Knit to last 14 sts, k1 tbl, k1, [yo, p2tog] four times, k1, k1 tbl, k2.
Round 32: Knit to last 14 sts, k1 tbl, p1, [k2tog, yo] four times, p1, k1 tbl, k2.
Rep the last 2 rounds five times, then Round 31 once. Work measures about 15cm (6in) from cast on.
Inc round: K1, m1, knit to last 17 sts, m1, k3, k1 tbl, p1, [k2tog, yo] four times, p1, k1 tbl, k2 (2 sts inc).
Work 4 rounds straight.
Next round: Knit to last 14 sts, k1 tbl, k1, [yo, p2 tog] four times, k1, k1 tbl, k2.
Next round: Knit to last 14 sts, k1 tbl, p1, [k2tog, yo] four times, p1, k1 tbl, k2.
Rep the last 2 rounds once.

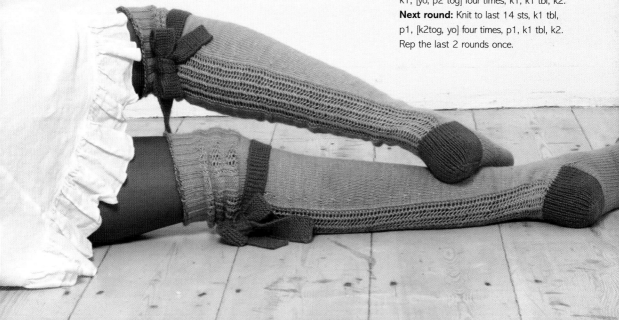

Inc round: K1, m1, knit to last 17 sts, m1, k3, k1 tbl, k1, [yo, p2 tog] four times, k1, k1 tbl, k2, (2 sts inc).
Work 4 rounds straight.
Next round: Knit to last 14 sts, k1 tbl, p1, [k2tog, yo] four times, p1, k1 tbl, k2.
Next round: Knit to last 14 sts, k1 tbl, k1, [yo, p2 tog] four times, k1, k1 tbl, k2.
Rep the last 2 rounds once.
Inc round: K1, m1, knit to last 17 sts, m1, k3, k1 tbl, p1, [k2tog, yo] four times, p1, k1 tbl, k2 (2 sts inc; 86 sts).
Work 7 rounds straight; work should measure 19.5cm (7¾in) from cast on.
Dec round: K2tog, knit to last 18 sts, skpo, k2, k1 tbl, p1, [k2tog, yo] four times, p1, k1 tbl, k2 (2 sts dec; 84 sts).
Work 7 rounds straight.
Rep last 8 rounds seventeen times more. (50 sts)
Work 6 rounds straight. Work should measure 56cm (22in) from cast on.
Next round: Knit to end of round.
Next round: Knit to last 21 sts.

HEEL FLAP

Place next 26 sts (unworked 21 sts from end of round and first 5 sts of this round, on other side of faggoted section) onto one needle to work for heel; 12 sts of faggoted section [k1 tbl, p1, [k2tog, yo] four times, p1, k1 tbl] should be situated in centre of heel needle, with 7 sts added on each side = 26 sts.

Place rem 24 sts on two needles to be worked later for instep.
The heel is worked in double strand of A to add extra padding and reinforce it.
Work 26 heel sts back and forth in rows as follows:
Row 1 (RS): Sl1, k25.
Row 2 (WS): Sl1, p25.
Rep Rows 1–2 until a total of 26 rows have been worked, ending with a WS row (13 chain sts along each edge of heel flap).

TURN HEEL

Work short rows as follows:
Row 1 (RS): Sl1, k13, k2tog, turn.
Row 2 (WS): Sl1, p2, p2tog, turn.
Row 3: Sl1, k2, k2tog, turn.
Row 4: Sl1, p2, p2tog, turn.
Rep Rows 3–4 until all heel sts have been worked; 4 heel sts rem.
Cut off both strands of A, leaving enough length on each end to sew in later.

GUSSETS

Rejoin MC for working in the round as follows:
Round 1: N1 – pick up 13 sts along side of Heel Flap, then work 2 sts of heel; N2 – work 2 rem sts of heel, then pick up 13 sts along other side of Heel Flap; N3 – work first 12 sts of instep; N4 – work rem 12 sts of instep. (54 sts)
Round begins at side of heel.

Round 2: Knit to last st on N4, transfer last st on to N1.
Round 3: N1 – skpo, knit to end (note that last st from N4 now rem on N1); N2 – knit to last st, transfer this st to N3; N3 – k2tog, knit to end; N4 – knit all sts (2 sts dec).
Round 4: Knit to end of round.
Round 5: N1 – skpo, knit to end; N2 – knit to last st, transfer this st to N3; N3 – k2tog, knit to end; N4 – knit all sts (2 sts dec; 50 sts).
Place marker between first and second sts on N1.

FOOT

Work straight in St st until foot measures 17.5cm (7in) from back of heel, or 6.5cm (2½in) less than desired total length.
To preserve the symmetry between underside and upper of foot section, slip the first st on N1 back onto N4; once this is done you should have 25 sts in total on N1 and N2, and 25 sts in total on N3 and N4.
To prepare for working toe, knit to end of N1. Cut off MC, leaving a 30cm (12in) tail. From now on, round begins at back of heel.

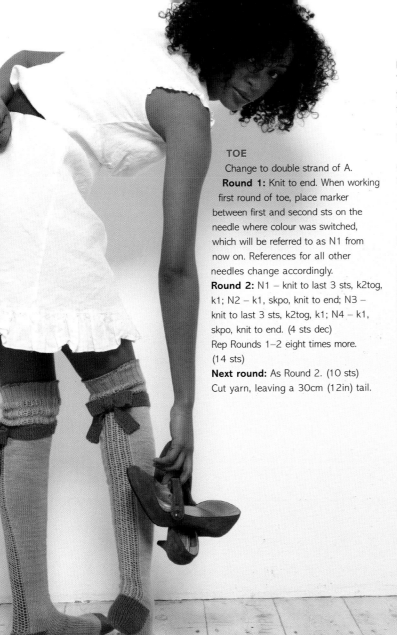

TOE

Change to double strand of A.

Round 1: Knit to end. When working first round of toe, place marker between first and second sts on the needle where colour was switched, which will be referred to as N1 from now on. References for all other needles change accordingly.

Round 2: N1 – knit to last 3 sts, k2tog, k1; N2 – k1, skpo, knit to end; N3 – knit to last 3 sts, k2tog, k1; N4 – k1, skpo, knit to end. (4 sts dec)
Rep Rounds 1–2 eight times more. (14 sts)

Next round: As Round 2. (10 sts)
Cut yarn, leaving a 30cm (12in) tail.

FINISHING

Thread tail on a tapestry needle, draw through rem sts and then pull up snugly to close end of toe. Sew in all loose ends. Block finished socks on sock blockers or press under a damp towel.

GARTERS (MAKE 2)

With A, cast on 9 sts. Work garter st (knit every row) until work measures 70cm (28in) from beg.
Cast (bind) off all sts. Sew in all loose ends.

SHE'S GOT LEGS!

- Try Rowan 4-ply Soft for a more basic and warmer version. You will need to double-check your tension (gauge).
- It's helpful to take note of the faggoted panel sequence and have it to hand for reference until you memorise it.
- This pattern can be made in plain stocking (stockinette) stitch with a k2, p2 rib cuff, omitting the decorative faggoted section. This is especially advised for adventurous beginners who would like to learn how to make stockings, because there isn't the added difficulty of working a complex lace pattern.

DESIGNED BY

Claire Garland

Lace Anklet Socks

Delicate lacy ankle socks, made in pure silk, are decorated with a pretty daisy motif that has tiny beads added to the 'eye' for an extra sparkly touch.

YARN

Debbie Bliss Pure Silk (100% silk), approx. 50g (1¾oz)/125m (137yd) per ball
  Two balls of Amethyst 08

HOOK

One 4.00mm (G/6) crochet hook

EXTRAS

Tapestry needle
Six glass-effect droplet beads
Removable stitch marker (or use short length of waste yarn)

TENSION (GAUGE)

20 sts and 22 rounds = 10cm (4in) square over double (single) crochet using 4.00mm (G/6) hook.

TO FIT

Women's shoe size 4–6 (US 6–8)

SKILL LEVEL

Intermediate/advanced

SOCKS (MAKE 2)
TOE
Foundation chain (RS): Make 4 ch.
Round 1: Working over the tail end, 8 dc (sc) in fourth ch from hook. Place marker to indicate start of round.
Round 2: *2 dc (sc) into each dc (sc); rep from * around. (16 dc (sc))
Round 3: As Round 2. (32 dc (sc))
Round 4: 1 dc (sc) into each dc (sc) around.
Round 5: *1 dc (sc) into each of next 3 dc (sc), 2 dc (sc) into next dc (sc); rep from * seven times more around. (40 dc (sc))
Round 6: 1 dc (sc) into each dc (sc) around.
Rep round 6 eight times more.

SHAPE SOCK SOLE AND SIDES
Cont to work in rows along sides and sole of the sock.
Row 16: 1 dc (sc) into each of next 12 dc (sc), 1 ch, turn.
Row 17: 1 dc (sc) into each of next 24 dc (sc), 1 ch, turn.
Rep last row fifteen times more.
Row 32: 1 dc (sc) into each of next 24 dc (sc), fasten off, ending on a WS row, then cont with heel shaping after completing Daisy Square.

DAISY SQUARE

Foundation chain (RS): Make 5 ch and join in with ss (sl st) to make a ring.

Round 1: 12 dc (sc) into ring, 1 ss (sl st) into first dc (sc) of round.

Round 2: [11 ch, 1 ss (sl st) into next dc (sc)] twelve times.

Round 3: 1 ss (sl st) into each of first 6 ch of first ch loop, 4 ch, 1 dc (sc) into sixth ch of next loop, 4 ch, [tr3tog (dc3tog), 4 ch, tr3tog (dc3tog)] into next loop, *4 ch, [1 tr (dc) into sixth ch of next loop, 4 ch] twice, [tr3tog (dc3tog), 4 ch, tr3tog (dc3tog)] into next loop; rep from * twice more, 4 ch, 1 dc (sc) into same place as sixth ss (sl st) at beg of round.

Round 4: 1 ss (sl st) into each of next 2 ch, 3 ch, tr2tog (dc2tog) into same 4 ch sp, 4 ch, 1 dc (sc) into next 4 ch sp, 4 ch, [tr3tog (dc3tog), 4 ch, tr3tog (dc3tog)] into 4 ch sp at corner; rep from * twice, 4 ch, 1 dc (sc) into next 4 ch sp, 4 ch, 1 ss (sl st) into third of 3 ch at beg of round. Fasten off. Sew in all loose ends.

SEW DAISY SQUARE ONTO SOCK

With RS of sock facing, ease the RS of the Daisy Square against the three straight edges of the sock upper. Join with small, neat, oversewn stitches. Sew in all loose ends.

SOCK HEEL

With RS shoe sole facing, rejoin yarn to first dc (sc) of Row 32. Place marker.**

Row 33: 1 dc (sc) into each of next 24 dc (sc), 1 ch, turn.
Rep row 33 twice more.

Row 36: 1 ch, 1 dc (sc) into 1 ch, 1 dc (sc) into each of next dc (sc), 2 dc (sc) into last dc (sc). (26 dc (sc))
Rep last 4 rows twice more. (30 dc (sc))

Row 45: 1dc (sc) into each of next 30 dc (sc), 1 ch, turn.
Rep last row twice more. Fasten off.
Fold last row (heel end) in half with WS together and join heel seam.

TRIM

Row 1: With RS facing and beginning at marker**, join in yarn and work 1 row of dc (sc) along heel edge, 1 ch, turn. (25 dc (sc))

Row 2: 1 dc (sc) into each dc (sc) along, turn.

Row 3: *Miss 1 dc (sc), 5 tr (dc) into next dc (sc), miss 1 dc (sc), 1 dc (sc) into next dc (sc); rep from *, ending 1 dc (sc) in last dc (sc).
Fasten off. Sew in all loose ends.
Sew three beads to the flower centre.

SIZE MATTERS

This size will fit a ladies' shoe size foot size 4–6 (US 6–8). For larger sizes, work Row 32 twice more for each pair of sizes. For example, work 34 rows for size 7–8 (US 9–10). Likewise, if a smaller size than a 4 (US 6) is needed, work two fewer rows.

LOVE THIS? Try knitting the Ribbon Wrist-Warmers by Sue Bradley on page 28.

DESIGNED BY

Ellen Mallett

Ribbon Socks

Soft velvet ribbon threaded up these girly socks adds extra texture to the design. For a bolder statement, knit in strong, contrasting colours.

YARN

Rowan 4-ply Soft (100% merino), approx. 50g (1¾oz)/ 175m (191yd) per ball

  Two balls of Fairy 395 **(MC)**

  One ball of Dove 394 **(A)**

NEEDLES

Set of five 2.75mm (US 2) double-pointed needles (dpns)

EXTRAS

Tapestry needle

90cm (1yd) of pink velvet ribbon

TENSION (GAUGE)

34 sts and 48 rows = 10cm (4in) square measured over St st using 2.75mm (US 2) needles.

TO FIT

Women's shoe size 4–6 (US 6–8)

SKILL LEVEL

Intermediate

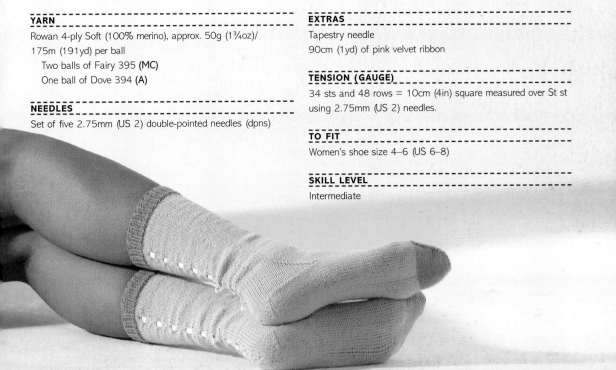

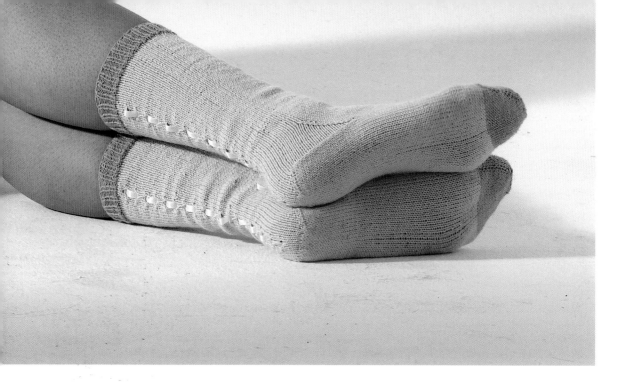

SOCKS (MAKE 2)
TOE AND FOOT

Using A, cast on 8 sts on one needle using loop cast on. Turn needle so bottom loops are on top and knit into them, knitting first 4 loops onto another needle and next 4 onto a third. (16 sts)

Knit 8 sts on needle 1 (N1) for front of sock.

Round 1: N1 – k1, m1, knit to end; N2 – knit to last stitch, m1, k1; N3 – k1, m1, knit to last stitch on needle, m1, k1.

Round 2: Knit.

Rep these two rounds until there are 60 sts on needles.

Change to MC and knit for 15cm (6in).

HEEL

Place 30 sts back onto one needle and work back and forth:

Row 1: Sl1, knit across.

Row 2: Sl1, purl across.

Rep until there are 30 heel flap rows, ending with a purl row.

Row 1: Sl1, k15, k2tog, k1, turn.

Row 2: Sl1, p5, p2tog, p1, turn.

Row 3: Sl1, k6, k2tog, k1, turn.

Row 4: Sl1, p7, p2tog, p1, turn.

Rep Rows 3–4, inc the sts worked by one each time until all side sts are used, ending with a knit row. (18 sts)

GUSSET

Round 1: Pick up and knit 15 sts along side of heel flap plus 1 st in gusset corner, knit across 30 sts on needle at front of sock, pick up and knit 1 st in gusset corner and 15 sts along side of heel flap, knit across 18 sts of sock back. (80 sts on four dpns)

LEG

Round 1: Knit.
Round 2: N1 – knit to last 2 sts, k2tog; N2 – knit; N3 – sl1, k1, psso, knit to end; N4 – knit. At the same time on next and every foll 6th round; N4 – k9, yo, k2tog, knit to end. Cont dec until there are 60 sts. Work in St st with yos as set until you reach 11cm (4¼ in) from first hole.

CALVES

Next yo round: Knit to 1 st before middle of back, m1, k1, yo, k2tog, m1, knit to end. (66 sts)
Cont knitting as set, inc 2 sts every 3rd yo round, until there are 20 yos up back of sock.

CUFF

Knit in MC to centre back – this now becomes end of each round.
Move sts onto three needles and work 1 row knit in A.
Work 13 more rows in k1, p1 rib.
Using a larger needle, if necessary, cast (bind) off loosely in rib.

FINISHING

Sew in all loose ends. Lightly block sock. Thread velvet ribbon through yos and stitch in place at bottom and top.

MADE TO MEASURE

- Toe-up socks can be tried on as you go and customised to fit – the pattern is for shoe size 4–6 (US 6–8). If your feet are wide, you can increase the toe a couple more times – each increase adds 4 sts – then adjust the numbers throughout the pattern. The length between toe and heel can be determined by measuring your foot and subtracting 10.5cm (4¼ in).
- If you have deeper or shorter heels than average, you can also adjust but again you will need to rewrite the numbers. This pattern increases from 60 sts after the ankle to 66 for the calf – if you need to increase more, add 2 sts on every other hole instead of every third. Remember that you need to knit an even number of yos for the velvet seam.
- Size 7–9 (US 9–12) would require three balls of MC; anything larger, four balls.

DESIGNED BY

Crown Slippers

The rich gold yarn pattern adds gleam and glam to these unusual slippers. For even more glamour, sew on crystal beads instead of – or as well as – the sequins!

YARN

Rowan Pure Wool DK (100% superwash wool), approx. 50g (1¾oz)/125m (137yd) per ball
   Two balls of Black 004 **(MC)**
Twilley's Goldfingering (80% viscose, 20% metallised polyester), approx. 50g (1¾oz)/200m (219yd) per ball
   Two balls of Gold 02 **(A)**

NEEDLES

Pair of 4.00mm (US 6) knitting needles

EXTRAS

100 multicoloured sequins
Tapestry needle

TENSION (GAUGE)

23 sts and 32 rows = 10cm (4in) square measured over St st using 4.00mm (US 6) needles.

TO FIT

One size

SKILL LEVEL

Advanced

SLIPPERS

ANKLE PIECES (MAKE 2)

Using MC, cast on 80 sts.
Beg at bottom of ankle, work in St st
as follows:

Rows 1–6: With MC.
Rows 7–8: With A.
Rows 9–10: With MC.
Row 11: Work bobble as follows:
k1 with MC; *with A, (k1, p1, k1, p1,
k1) into next st, sl second, third, fourth
and fifth sts over first st on needle
(1 st in A rem on needle); k3 with MC,
rep from * across row to last 3 sts, work
bobble in next st, k2, carrying A loosely
across back of work.
Purl 1 row with MC.
Beg chart and work until complete,
remembering to work last 4 rows in
chart as garter st (indicated by 'x' in
squares).
Cast (bind) off firmly but not tightly.

SLIPPER SOLES (MAKE 2)

Using MC, cast on 14 sts.
Row 1: Knit.
Row 2: Purl.
Row 3: Kfb, k to last st, kfb.
Row 4: Purl.
Rows 5–10: Rep Rows 3–4 three
times more.
Rows 11–24: Work in St st. (22 sts)
Row 25: Skpo, k to last 2 sts, k2tog.
Rows 26–28: Work in St st.
Row 29: As Row 25.

Rows 30–40: Work in St st; work
should now be 12.5cm (5in) long.
Row 41: Kfb, k to last st, kfb.
Row 42: Purl.
Rows 43–48: Rep Rows 41–42 three
times more.
Rows 49–70: Work in St st. (26 sts)
Row 71: Skpo, knit to last 2 sts, k2tog.
Row 72: Purl; work should now be
22.5cm (9in).
Rep Rows 71–72, then row 71
once more.
Row 76: P2tog, purl to last 2 sts,
p2tog tbl.
Row 77: Skpo, knit to last 2 sts, k2tog.
Row 78: As Row 76.
Cast (bind) off rem 14 sts.

LEFT SIDE OF SLIPPER FOOT (MAKE 2)

Using MC, cast on 16 sts.
Row 1: Knit.
Row 2: Purl.
Rows 3–32: Cont in St st; work should
now be 10cm (4in).
Row 33: Kfb, knit to end.
Row 34: Purl.
Row 35: Knit.
Row 36: Purl.
Rows 37–46: Rep Rows 33–36 twice.
(19 sts)
Row 47: Knit to last 2 sts, k2tog.
Row 48: Purl.
Row 49: As Row 33.
Row 50: Purl.
Row 51: Kfb, knit to last 2 sts, k2tog.

STRAIGHT WEAVE

- When working with both yarns in
  the same row, weave A at the
  back of the work when not in use.
  Use separate small balls of B for
  each segment of crown and do
  not weave across the back.
- To make smaller slippers, use
  3.75mm (US 5) needles; for a
  larger size, use 4.50mm (US 7) –
  this will alter the tension (gauge).

Rows 52–54: Work in St st.
Row 55: Knit to last 2 sts, k2tog.
Rows 56–58: Work in St st.
Rows 59–70: Rep Rows 55–58
three times.
Rows 71–78: Rep Rows 55–56
four times.
Row 79: Knit to last 2 sts, k2tog.
Row 80: P2tog, purl to end of row.
Rows 81–86: Rep Rows 79–80
three times.
Cast (bind) off rem 3 sts.

RIGHT SIDE OF SLIPPER FOOT (MAKE 2)

Knit as for left side, reversing
all shapings.

FINISHING

Sew in all loose ends and press pieces lightly. Sew slipper foot pieces together along centre front seam using one left and one right side, sewing along the straight seam from toe to the beginning of the shaping. Sew the centre back seam of the slipper foot pieces. Sew the slipper sole to the bottom edge of the slipper foot. Sew the side seams of each ankle piece together to make a 'cuff'. Sew round the bottom edge of the ankle piece, joining it to the slipper foot. Make sure the back seams line up with each other. Decorate with sequins, using photograph as a guide for placement.

Key

- ☐ A
- ■ MC
- ☒ MC using garter stitch

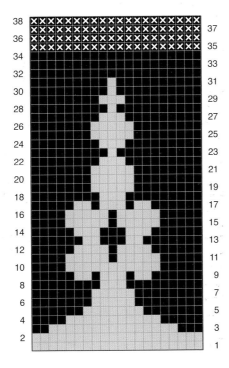

DESIGNED BY

Tanis Gray

Cable Leg-Warmers

These chunky cable leg-warmers will keep you feeling really cosy on the very coldest days. Working up quickly, they are an ideal introduction to the cable technique.

YARN

Rowan Big Wool (100% merino wool), approx. 100g (3½ oz)/80m (87yd) per ball
  Four balls of Flirty 038

NEEDLES

Set of four 10.00mm (US 15)
double-pointed needles (dpns)

EXTRAS

Tapestry needle
Cable needle

TENSION (GAUGE)

10 sts and 12 rows = 10cm (4in) square measured over cable pattern using 10.00mm (US 15) needles.

TO FIT

Women's size small, with thigh measuring approx. 38cm (15in). Stitches can be added between cable columns to increase the size.

SKILL LEVEL

Beginner

SPECIAL ABBREVIATIONS

See page 254 for information on C4L.

LEG-WARMERS (MAKE 2)

Cast on 26 sts, dividing sts evenly across dpns.

Rounds 1–10: [K1, p1] to end.

Round 11: [K4, p1] to last 2 sts, p2tog.

Rounds 12–13: [K4, p1] to end.

Round 14: [C4L, p1] to end.

Rounds 15–19: As Round 12.

Rep Rounds 14–19 until 39 rounds have been worked.

Round 40 (cable round): [C4L, p1, kfb] to end. (30 sts)

Rounds 41–45: [K4, p2] to end.

Round 46: [C4L, p2] to end.

Rep Rounds 41–46 until Round 69.

Round 70 (cable round): [C4L, p2, kfb] to end. (35 sts)

Rounds 71–73: [K4, p3] to end.

Round 74: [K1, p1] to last 2 sts, p2tog.

Rounds 75–84: [K1, p1] to end.

Cast (bind) off loosely. Sew in all loose ends.

RING THE CHANGES

• Try substituting Debbie Bliss Cashmerino Super Chunky in Sage 23 – but remember to adjust the tension (gauge) slightly.

• For a variation on the pattern, knit to directly under the knee and cast (bind) off for a shorter version, lessening the length of ribbing, or add another colour and make stripes.

• Do not cast (bind) off too tightly, as then the leg-warmers might cut off your circulation!

• Do not cast (bind) off too loosely, as then the leg-warmers might slide right down the leg!

DESIGNED BY

Flip-Flop Socks

Get that beach holiday feeling even in the depths of winter! Wear your flip-flops all year round with these carefree socks with a separate big toe.

YARN
Rowan Wool Cotton (50% merino wool, 50% cotton), approx. 50g(1¾oz)/ 113m (124yd) per ball
    Two balls of Plum 910

NEEDLES
Set of four 3.50mm (US 4) double-pointed needles (dpns)

EXTRAS
Stitch marker
Stitch holder
Tapestry needle

TENSION (GAUGE)
24 sts and 33 rows = 10cm (4in) square measured over St st using 3.50mm (US 4) needles.

TO FIT
One size

SKILL LEVEL
Intermediate

SOCKS
RIGHT FOOT
Using Continental method, cast on 52 sts and divide them so there are 16 sts on first needle and 18 sts on the other two needles.
Join, making sure sts are not twisted. PM for beg of round.
Work in k2, p2 rib for 5cm (2in).

CHANGE TO PATT
Round 1: Knit.
Round 2: [P1, k3] to end.
Round 3: Knit.
Round 4: K2 [p1, k3] to last 2 sts, p1, k1.
Rep Rounds 1–4 once more.

HEEL FLAP
Row 1: Sl1, k25, turn.
Row 2: Sl1, p25, turn.
Cont to work across these 26 sts.
Row 3: [Sl1, k1] to end of row.
Row 4: Sl1, p to end of row.
Rep last 2 rows thirteen times more (30 rows in all). Remove marker.

TURN HEEL
Row 31: Sl1, k15, k2tog, k1, turn.
Row 32: Sl1, p7, p2tog, p1, turn.
Row 33: Sl1, k8, k2tog, k1, turn.
Row 34: Sl1, p9, p2tog, p1, turn.
Row 35: Sl1, k10, k2tog, k1, turn.
Row 36: Sl1, p11, p2tog, p1, turn.
Row 37: Sl1, k12, k2tog, k1, turn.
Row 38: Sl1, p13, p2tog, p1, turn.
Row 39: Sl1, k14, k2tog, k1, turn.
Row 40: Sl1, p14, p2tog, turn.
On N1, knit across 16 sts, then pick up 15 sts down side edge of heel flap.
On N2, knit next 26 sts.
On N3, pick up 15 sts up other side edge of heel flap, k8 from N1.

GUSSET
Round 1: N1 – knit to last 3 sts, k2tog, k1; N2 – k2, [p1, k3] to end; N3 – k1, ssk, knit to end.
Round 2: Knit.
Round 3: N1 – knit to last 3 sts, k2tog, k1; N2 – [p1, k3] to last 2 sts, p1, k1; N3 – k1, ssk, knit to end.
Round 4: Knit.
Rep Rounds 1–4 four times more.
(13 sts on N1 and N3)

INSTEP
Round 1: K13, [p1, k3] to end of N2, k13.
Round 2: Knit.
Round 3: K13, k2, [p1, k3] to last 2 sts of N2, p1, k1, k13.
Round 4: Knit.
Rep Rounds 1–4 until sock measures 22.5cm (9in) along sole from heel turn, or until this measurement is the length of your foot less 2.5cm (1in). Finish at end of N2.

RIGHT FOOT TOE SHAPING

Work big toe separately as follows:

Next round: K7, turn, cast on 2 sts, turn, leave next 38 sts on stitch holder, knit last 7 sts from N2. Distribute these 16 sts across three needles.

Knit 10 rounds.

Next 2 rounds: K2tog to end of round. Cut yarn and draw end through rem 4 sts, pulling tight to close gap.

Rejoin yarn at base of big toe and return sts from holder to dpns. Work rest of toes as follows:

Next round: N1 – k16, k2tog, k1; N2 – k1, ssk, k12; N3 – k4, pick up 2 sts at base of big toe (2 sts cast on previously), k4.

Continue to dec as foll:

Next round: N1 – knit to last 3 sts, k2tog, k1; N2 – k1, ssk, knit to end; N3 – knit.

Cont dec in same way on every round until 20 sts rem.

Next 2 rounds: Dec as before on N1 and N2. At the same time, dec on N3 as follows: k1, ssk, knit to last 3 sts, k2tog, k1. (12 sts)

Next round: Slip last 3 sts onto new needle, then k3 from N1. On next needle, k3 from N2, then last 3 sts from N3 (sts now on two needles).

Sew stitches together using Kitchener stitch (see page 256) or use three-needle cast (bind) off (see page 255).

LEFT FOOT

Work as for right foot until toe shaping.

LEFT FOOT TOE SHAPING

Work big toe separately as follows:

Next round: K19, leave these sts on holder, k14, turn, cast on 2 sts, turn, leave rem 19 sts on stitch holder. Distribute these 16 sts across three needles.

Knit 10 rounds.

Next 2 rounds: K2tog to end of round. Cut off yarn, draw end through rem 4 sts and pull tightly to close gap.

Rejoin yarn at base of big toe and restore stitches from holder to dpns. Work rest of toes as follows:

Next round: N1 – k16, k2tog, k1; N2 – k1, ssk, k12; N3 – k4, pick up 2 sts at base of big toe (2 sts cast on previously), k4.

Cont to dec as follows:

Next round: N1 – knit to last 3 sts, k2tog, k1; N2 – k1, ssk, knit to end; N3 – knit.

Cont to dec in same way on every round until 20 sts rem.

Next 2 rounds: Cont to dec as before on N1 and N2. At the same time, dec on N3 as follows: k1, ssk, knit to last 3 sts, k2tog, k1. (12 sts)

Next round: Slip last 3 sts onto new needle, k3 from N1. On next needle, k3 from N2, then last 3 sts from N3 (sts now on two needles).

Sew stitches together using Kitchener stitch (see page 256) or use three-needle cast (bind) off (see page 255).

FINISHING

Sew in all loose ends. Press lightly as per ball-band instructions.

DESIGNED BY

Hound's-Tooth Socks

A black-and-white hound's-tooth print makes a striking statement on these calf-length socks. For a different look, work a longer rib and turn over to form a cuff.

YARN

Rowan Scottish Tweed 4-ply (100% wool), approx.
25g (1oz)/110m (120yd) per ball
  Three balls of Midnight 023 (MC)
  Two balls of Porridge 024 (A)

NEEDLES

Set of four 3.25mm (US 3) double-pointed needles (dpns)
Set of four 2.75mm (US 2) double-pointed needles (dpns)

EXTRAS

Stitch marker
Tapestry needle

TENSION (GAUGE)

28 sts and 32 rows = 10cm (4in) square measured over hound's-tooth check in St st using 3.25mm (US 3) needles.

TO FIT

One size

SKILL LEVEL

Intermediate

SPECIAL ABBREVIATIONS

See pages 254–255 for information on lk2tog, lp2tog and three-needle cast (bind) off.

SOCKS (MAKE 2)

Using 2.75mm (US 2) needles and MC, cast on 64 sts.

Place 21 sts on each of the first two needles and 22 sts on the third.

Work 3cm (1¼in) in k1, p1 rib, dec 1 st at end of last round. (63 sts)

Change to 3.25mm (US 3) needles and begin working in St st.

WORK HOUND'S-TOOTH CHECK PATT

Join in A and, starting with Round 1, foll the chart until six reps of the patt (48 rows) have been completed and sock measures 17.5cm (7in) from cast-on edge.

DIVIDE FOR HEEL AND INSTEP

With MC only, k32. Arrange these 32 sts on a single needle and cont in MC on these sts only for the heel.

HEEL

Row 1 (WS facing): Sl1p, p31 (to end of needle), turn.

Row 2: Sl1, k30 (1 st rem), turn.

Row 3: Sl1p, p29 (1 st rem), turn.

Row 4: Sl1, k28 (2 sts rem), turn.

Row 5: Sl1p, p27 (2 sts rem), turn.

Row 6: Sl1, k26 (3 sts rem), turn.

Row 7: Sl1p, p25 (3 sts rem), turn.

Row 8: Sl1, k24 (4 sts rem), turn.

Row 9: Sl1p, p23 (4 sts rem), turn.

Row 10: Sl1, k22 (5 sts rem), turn.

Row 11: Sl1p, p21 (5 sts rem), turn.

Row 12: Sl1, k20 (6 sts rem), turn.

Row 13: Sl1p, p19 (6 sts rem), turn.

Row 14: Sl1, k18 (7 sts rem), turn.

Row 15: Sl1p, p17 (7 sts rem), turn.

Row 16: Sl1, k16 (8 sts rem), turn.

Row 17: Sl1p, p15 (8 sts rem), turn.

Row 18: Sl1, k14 (9 sts rem), turn.

Row 19: Sl1p, p13 (9 sts rem), turn.

Row 20: Sl1, k12 (10 sts rem), turn.

Row 21: Sl1p, p11 (10 sts rem), turn.

Row 22: Sl1, k10, lk2tog (10 sts rem on LH needle), turn.

Row 23: Sl1p, p10, lp2tog (10 sts rem on LH needle), turn.

Row 24: Sl1, k11, lk2tog (9 sts rem), turn.

Row 25: Sl1p, p12, lp2tog (9 sts rem), turn.

Row 26: Sl1, k13, lk2tog (8 sts rem), turn.

Row 27: Sl1p, p14, lp2tog (8 sts rem), turn.

Row 28: Sl1, k15, lk2tog (7 sts rem), turn.

Row 29: Sl1p, p16, lp2tog (7 sts rem), turn.

Row 30: Sl1, k17, lk2tog (6 sts rem), turn.

Row 31: Sl1p, p18, lp2tog (6 sts rem), turn.

Row 32: Sl1, k19, lk2tog (5 sts rem), turn.

Row 33: Sl1p, p20, lp2tog (5 sts rem), turn.

Row 34: Sl1, k21, lk2tog (4 sts rem), turn.

Row 35: Sl1p, p22, lp2tog (4 sts rem), turn.

Row 36: Sl1, k23, lk2tog (3 sts rem), turn.

Row 37: Sl1p, p24, lp2tog (3 sts rem), turn.

Row 38: Sl1, k25, lk2tog (2 sts rem), turn.

Row 39: Sl1p, p26, lp2tog (2 sts rem), turn.

Row 40: Sl1, k27, lk2tog (1 st rem), turn.

Row 41: Sl1p, p28, lp2tog (1 st rem), turn.

Row 42: Sl1, k29, lk2tog (no st rem), turn.

Row 43: Sl1p, p30, lp2tog (no st rem), turn.

Rearrange these sts so the first 21 sts rem on first needle and the remaining 11 sts are slipped onto second needle. There should now be 21 sts on each needle.

Working with both colours and starting with Round 1, work in hound's-tooth patt foll chart until six reps of the patt (48 rows) have been completed.

SHAPE TOE

Cut off A and cont in MC only.

Round 1: K1, skpo, k12, k2tog, k12, k2tog, k2, skpo, k25, k2tog, k1.

Round 2: K29, PM on needle, k29 (to end of round).

Round 3: K1, skpo, knit to 3 sts before marker, k2tog, k1, SM, k1, skpo, knit to 3 sts before end of round, k2tog, k1.

Round 4: Knit, SM.

Rounds 5–12: Rep last 2 rounds four times more. (38 sts)

Round 13: As Round 3.

Rounds 14–16: Rep Round 3 three times more. (22 sts)

Slip the first 11 sts onto one needle and the remaining 11 sts onto a second needle. Sew together using Kitchener st (see page 256) or use three-needle cast (bind) off.

FINISHING

Sew in all loose ends and block lightly.

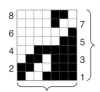

Key

■ MC
□ A

NOTEWORTHY

- For an elastic edge, try casting on over two needles held together, knitting into the back of each stitch to form the next loop. This will give a twisted stitch on the first row.

- When knitting in the round, all rounds are right side, so always read the chart from right to left.

- From Row 22 onwards, turning the short-row heel can be simplified by working the stated number of sts plus 1, then turning. For example, Row 22 would read: 'Sl1, k11, turn'. This will leave holes, but they could be darned in at the end.

- It is difficult to prevent a little hole appearing at the join of the heel with the top of the sock. If this occurs, gently pull up the threads on the inside and carefully darn them in.

DESIGNED BY

Textured Socks with Flowers

A pretty bouquet of leaves and flowers at the ankle lend flirty detail to these easy-going socks.

YARN

Rowan Wool Cotton (50% merino wool, 50% cotton), approx. 50g (1¾oz)/113m (124yd) per ball

    Three balls of Pumpkin 962 **(MC)**

    One ball of Rich 911 **(A)**

    One ball of Deepest Olive 907 **(B)**

NEEDLES

Set of five 2.75mm (US 2) double-pointed needles (dpns)

One 3.50mm (E/4) crochet hook

EXTRAS

Stitch marker

Tapestry needle

Sewing needle

24 drop beads

24 green 6/0 E beads

30 orange-yellow 6/0 E beads

TENSION (GAUGE)

5½ sts and 8 rows = 2.5cm (1in) square measured over St st using 2.75mm (US 2) needles.

TO FIT

One size

SKILL LEVEL

Intermediate

SOCKS (MAKE 2)

CUFF

Using 2.75mm (US 2) needles and MC, cast on 48 sts and divide them equally across four dpns (12 sts on each). Join into circle without twisting the sts. Place marker to indicate beg of round.

Round 1: [K2, p2] to end.

Rounds 2–33: Cont in rib as set, or until cuff measures 11cm (4½in) from cast on.

LEG

Round 1: [Yo, k1, yo, sl1, k2tog, psso] to end.

Round 2: Knit.

Round 3: [Sl1, k2tog, psso, yo, k1, yo] to end.

Round 4: Knit.

Rep Rounds 1–4 until piece measures 25cm (10in) from beg.

Knit sts on first needle; leave sts on second and third needles on hold. From now you will work sts from fourth and first needles only.

HEEL FLAP

Put sts from first and fourth needles onto one needle. Now work in rows only.

Row 1 (WS): Purl.

Row 2: Sl1p wyb, knit to end.

Row 3: Sl1p wyf, purl to end.

Rep Rows 2–3 eight times more, or until the Heel Flap measures 5cm (2in).

TURN HEEL

Row 1 (RS): K14, ssk, k1, turn.

Row 2: Sl1, p5, p2tog, p1, turn.

Row 3: Sl1, k6, ssk, k1, turn.

Row 4: Sl1, p7, p2tog, p1, turn.

Row 5: Sl1, k8, ssk, k1, turn.

Row 6: Sl1, p9, p2tog, p1, turn.

Row 7: Sl1, k10, ssk, k1, turn.

Row 8: Sl1, p11, p2tog, p1, turn.

Row 9: Sl1, k12, ssk, turn.

Row 10: P13, p2tog, turn. (14 sts)

HEEL GUSSET

Set-up round (RS): K14, then with same needle pick up 10 sts along side of Heel Flap and 1 additional st beyond flap to close gap. (25 sts)

Work 24 sts over second and third needles with cellular patt as foll:

Next round: Yo, k2tog, yo, sl1, k2tog, psso, [yo, k1, yo, sl1, k2tog, psso]; rep to last 3 sts on third needle, yo, k1, yo, k2tog.

With fourth needle, pick up 1 st between third needle and Heel Flap to close gap, then pick up 10 sts along side of Heel Flap and k7 from first needle. Now you have four needles with 60 sts divided as foll: 18, 12, 12, 18 sts. Beg of round is the heel centre.

Round 1: Knit.

Round 2: N1 – knit; N2 and N3 – work cellular patt as foll: [yo, sl1, k2tog, psso, yo, k1]; rep to heel; N4 – knit.

FRINGE

Using 3.50mm (E/4) hook and MC, double (single) crochet around the edge of cuff. Fasten off. Sew in ends. Cut yarn A into pieces 12–15cm (4¾–6in) long, fold each piece in half and tie it to the edge of the cuff (space equally, with two ends coming out of each tie). Tie one end of each tie with one end of the adjacent tie into a knot; rep until all ends are tied into knots. Trim ends to the same lengths close to the knot.
Split a length of yarn in half, thread through sewing needle and sew beads to the cuff as foll: go through cuff edge, thread on 1 green bead and 1 drop bead, with needle go back through the same green bead, then go through edge creating a triangle (see photo); rep eleven times more. Sew in ends.

Round 3: N1 – knit to last 3 sts, k2tog, k1; N2 and N3 – knit; N4 – k1, ssk, knit to end (dec 4 sts).

Round 4: N1 – knit; N2 and N3 – work cellular patt as foll: yo, k2tog, yo, sl1, k2tog, psso, [yo, k1, yo, sl1, k2tog, psso]; rep to last 3 sts on N3, yo, k1, yo, k2tog; N4 – knit.

Round 5: As Round 3.

Rep Rounds 2–5 until you have 48 sts left, then work as foll:

Round 1: Knit.
Round 2: As Round 2 above.
Round 3: Knit.
Round 4: As Round 4 above.
Cont until foot measures 17.5cm (7in), or length of your foot less 2.5cm (2in), then start shaping toe.

SHAPE TOE
Rounds 1–2: Knit.
Round 3: N1 – knit to last 3 sts, k2tog, k1; N2 – k1, ssk, knit to end; N3 – as for N1; N4 – as for N2 (dec 4 sts).
Round 4: Knit.
Rounds 5–12: As Rounds 3–4. (28 sts)
Rounds 13–17: As Round 3. (8 sts)
Cut off yarn, thread it through sts and pull tight to close. Sew in end.

LARGE FLOWER (MAKE 2)
Using 2.75mm (US 2) needles and A, cast on 49 sts.
Rows 1–2: Knit.
Row 3: K1, *cast (bind) off 7 sts, leave the last cast-off (bound-off) st on RH needle; rep from * five times more. (7 sts)
Row 4: K7.
Cut off yarn, thread through live sts to close the round, then sew the sides to form flower.

SMALL FLOWER (MAKE 2)
Using 2.75mm (US 2) needles and A, cast on 21 sts.
Row 1: K1, *cast (bind) off 3 sts, leave the last cast-off (bound-off) st on RH needle; rep from * four times more. (6 sts)
Cut off yarn, thread through live sts to close the round, then sew the sides to form flower.

LEAVES (MAKE 6)
Using 2.75mm (US 2) needles and B, cast on 3 sts.
Row 1 (WS): Purl.
Row 2: K1, yo, k1, yo, k1. (5 sts)
Row 3: Purl.
Row 4: K2, yo, k1, yo, k2. (7 sts)
Row 5: Purl.
Row 6: Ssk, k3, k2tog. (5 sts)
Row 7: Purl.
Row 8: Ssk, k1, k2tog. (3 sts)
Row 9: Purl.
Row 10: K3tog.
Fasten off.

FINISHING
Arrange flowers and leaves, referring to photograph for positioning, and sew to socks. Split a length of yarn in half, thread through sewing needle and sew orange-yellow beads in centre of large flowers.

DESIGNED BY

Gypsy Flower Socks

Rediscover flower power with these bright floral socks, knitted using the intarsia technique. Twist the yarn when changing colour to prevent holes.

YARN

Rowan Scottish Tweed 4-ply (100% wool), approx. 25g (1oz)/110m (120yd) per ball

Three balls of Midnight 023 **(MC)**
One ball of Lavender 005 **(A)**
One ball of Gold 028 **(B)**
One ball of Brilliant Pink 010 **(C)**
One ball of Rust 009 **(D)**
One ball of Sunset 011 **(E)**

NEEDLES

Pair of 3.00mm (US 3) knitting needles
Pair of 2.75mm (US 2) knitting needles

EXTRAS

Three stitch holders

TENSION (GAUGE)

27 sts and 37 rows = 10cm (4in) square measured over St st intarsia patt using 3.00mm (US 3) needles.

TO FIT

One size

SKILL LEVEL

Intermediate

MOCK CABLE RIB

Row 1: *P2, twist 2 (by knitting into second st on LH needle, stretch st just made slightly, then knit into back of first st and sl both sts off needles); rep from * to last 2 sts, p2.
Row 2: [K2, p2] to last 2 sts, k2.
Row 3: [P2, k2] to last 2 sts, p2.
Row 4: As Row 2.
These 4 rows form the Mock Cable Rib patt.

BOBBLE

Kfb, turn, p2, turn, k2, turn, p2, turn, k2tog.

SOCKS (MAKE 2)

Using 2.75mm (US 2) needles and A, cast on 74 sts.
Work Row 2 of mock cable rib, beg with k2.
Change to B and work 5cm (2in) in mock cable rib, beg with row 1.
Change to 3.00mm (US 3) needles and work 26 sts in mock cable rib, k1, work 20 sts of chart, k1, work 26 sts in mock cable rib.
Cont as set until Row 48 of chart has been completed.

DIVIDE FOR HEEL AND INSTEP

Next row: Patt 55 sts, turn, placing rem 19 sts onto a stitch holder.
Next row: Patt 36 sts, turn, placing rem 19 sts onto a stitch holder.
Cont on these 36 sts in patt for 48 rows.

Place these sts onto a stitch holder. With RS facing, slip sts from previous two holders onto one needle, with back of leg seam at centre.
Work 20 rows in Mock Cable Rib.

TURN HEEL

Row 1: K28, skpo, turn.
Row 2: P19, p2tog, turn.
Row 3: K19, skpo, turn.
Row 4: As Row 2.
Rep last 2 rows until 20 sts rem, ending with a purl row, then pick up and purl 16 sts along side of heel flap onto same needle. (36 sts)
Next row: Knit to end, then pick up and knit 16 sts along side of heel flap. (52 sts)
Next row: Purl.

SHAPE INSTEP

Cont in St st.
Row 1: K1, skpo, knit to last 3 sts, k2tog, k1.
Row 2: K1, purl to last st, k1.
Rep last 2 rows until 40 sts rem, then cont in St st until foot section measures same as top section, ending with a WS row.
Next row: Work to end, then work in St st across 36 sts on spare needle. (76 sts)
Next row: Purl.

SHAPE TOE

Row 1: [K1, k2tog, k32, k2tog, k1] twice.
Row 2 and every alt row: Purl.
Row 3: [K1, k2tog, k30, k2tog, k1] twice.
Row 5: [K1, k2tog, k28, k2tog, k1] twice.
Cont dec in this way on alt rows until 32 sts rem, ending with a WS row.
Slip first 16 sts onto a spare needle, fold work in half with RS facing and sew sts tog using Kitchener stitch (see page 256).

FINISHING

Sew all loose ends into their own colour. Join the seams at the side of the foot and the seam at back of leg. Lightly press the parts knitted in St st only.

Key

- ■ MC
- ▨ A
- ▨ B
- ▨ C
- ■ D
- ▨ E
- ✤ Bobble

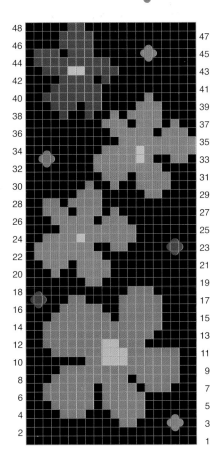

DESIGNED BY

Simona Merchant-Dest

Vandyke Lace Socks

These lacy socks in shocking raspberry feature a pretty scalloped edge and tie detail.

YARN

Rowan Wool Cotton (50% merino wool, 50% cotton), approx. 50g (1¾oz)/113m (124yd) per ball

Three balls of Flower 943

NEEDLES

Set of five 2.75mm (US 2) double-pointed needles (dpns)

One 2.00mm (B/1) crochet hook

One 3.25mm (D/3) crochet hook

EXTRAS

Two stitch markers

Tapestry needle

TENSION (GAUGE

6 sts and 9 rows = 2.5cm (1in) square measured over St st using 2.75mm (US 2) needles; 6 sts and 7.5 rows = 2.5cm (1in) square measured over Staggered Eyelet patt using 2.75mm (US 2) needles; 5.5 sts and 7.5 rows = 2.5cm (1in) square measured over Vandyke Lace patt using 2.75mm (US 2) needles.

TO FIT

One size

SKILL LEVEL

Advanced

SPECIAL ABBREVIATIONS

See page 254 for information on de.

SOCKS (MAKE 2 ALIKE TO BEG OF LEG)

TOE

Using 2.75mm (US 2) needles, cast on 8 sts on needle 1 (N1). Turn upside down, and with another dpn cast 7 sts onto the cast-on edge side, pulling sts through the spaces between the cast-on sts on N1. (15 sts)

Round 1: N1 – k4; N2 – k4; N3 – k1, m1, k2; N4 – k4 (16 sts; 4 sts on each needle). Place marker to denote beg of round.

Round 2: *N1 – k1, m1, knit to end; N2 – knit to last st, m1, k1; rep from * once more for N3 and N4. (20 sts)

Rounds 3–4: As Round 2. (28 sts)

Round 5: Knit.

Round 6: As Round 2.

Rounds 7–18: Rep Rounds 5–6 six times more. (56 sts)

Rounds 19–21: Knit; in the last round dec 1 st. (55 sts)

FOOT

Start working the Staggered Eyelet patt over N1 and N2; cont in St st over N3 and N4 as foll:

Round 1: [K2, k2tog, yo] six times, k3, knit to end of round.

Rounds 2–4: Knit.

Round 5: K4, [k2tog, yo, k2] five times, k3, knit to end of round.

Rounds 6–8: Knit.

Rep Rounds 1–8 five times more or until piece measures 17.5cm (7in) from toe, or your foot length less 5cm (2in). In the last round, work only to last st on N4, bring the yarn in front as if to purl and sl the last st. Now leave sts on N1 and N2 on hold and work the heel shaping over N3 and N4 only.

HEEL

Row 1 (WS): Slip first unworked st from left dpn to right dpn (wrapping that first st around its base with the working yarn), purl to last st, sl last st and bring yarn around to front, turn.

Row 2: Sl1, knit to last worked st, bring yarn in front and sl last worked st as if to purl, bring yarn around to back, turn.

Row 3: Sl1, purl to last worked st, sl1, wrap the yarn around, turn.

Rep Rows 2–3 until there are 10 worked sts left and 9 sl wrapped sts on each side.

TURNING HEEL

Row 1 (RS): Knit all worked sts to first unworked wrapped st, pick up st with wrap and knit them tog. Slip next unworked st and wrap yarn around, turn.

Row 2: Sl1 (double-wrapped) st and purl all worked sts, pick up wrap(s) and unworked st and purl them tog. Wrap the foll unworked st and sl it, turn.

Row 3: Sl1 (double-wrapped) st and knit all worked sts, pick up both wraps and unworked st and knit them tog. Slip next unworked st, wrap it around, turn. Cont in this fashion, rep Rows 2–3 until all unworked sts are worked, finishing with a WS row. (28 sts)

LEG

Start working over all dpns again.

Round 1: [K2, k2tog, yo] six times, k3, m1, k to end. (56 sts)

Rounds 2–4: Knit.

Round 5: [K2tog, yo, k2] to end.

Rounds 6–8: Knit.

Round 9: [K2, k2tog, yo] to end.

Rounds 10–12: Knit.

Round 13: As Round 5.

RIGHT SOCK

Rounds 14–16: Knit.

Round 17: *K2, k2tog, yo**; rep from * four times, k7, yo, ssk, k5, k2tog, yo; rep from * to ** five times to end.

Round 18: K19, PM, k17, PM, k20.

Note: Work Vandyke Lace patt between markers; work Staggered Eyelet patt before and after markers.

Round 19: K19, SM, k6, k2tog, yo, k1, yo, ssk, k6, SM, k20 to end.

Round 20 and each EVEN round: Knit.

Round 21: *K2tog, yo, k2**; rep from * three times, k3, SM, k5, k2tog, yo, k3, yo, ssk, k5, SM, k4; rep from * to ** four times to end.

Round 23: K19, SM, work de, k3, yo, ssk, k2, work de, SM, k20 to end.

Round 25: *K2, k2tog, yo**; rep from * three times, k3, SM, ***work de, k1; rep from *** once, work de, SM; rep from * to ** five times to end.

Round 27: K19, SM, work de, k2tog, yo, k3, yo, ssk, work de, SM, k20 to end.

Round 29: *K2tog, yo, k2**; rep from * three times, k3, SM, work de, k3, yo, ssk, k2, work de, SM, k4; rep from * to ** four times to end.

Round 31: K19, SM, ***work de, k1; rep from *** once, work de, SM, k20 to end.

Round 33: *K2, k2tog, yo**; rep from * three times, k3, SM, work de, k2tog, yo, k3, yo, ssk, work de, SM; rep from * to ** five times to end.

Round 35: As Round 23.

Round 37: *K2tog, yo, k2**; rep from * three times, k3, SM, ***work de, k1; rep from *** once, work de, SM, k4; rep from * to ** four times to end.

Round 39: As Round 27.

Round 41: *K2, k2tog, yo**; rep from * three times, k3, SM; work de, k3, yo, ssk, k2, work de, SM; rep from * to ** five times to end.

Round 43: As Round 31.

Round 45: *K2tog, yo, k2; rep from * three times, k3, SM, work de, k2tog, yo, k3, yo, ssk, work de, SM, k4; rep from * to ** four times to end.

Rounds 46–51: Knit.

Round 52: *K2, p2; rep from * to end.

Round 53: *K2, yo, p2tog, k2, p2, k2, p2tog, yo**; rep from * once, k2, yo, p2tog, k2, p2tog, yo; rep from * to ** twice to end.

Rounds 54–63: Cont in est rib patt *k2, p2; rep from * to end.

Rounds 64–65: Knit.

In next round, cast (bind) off all sts. Do NOT cut yarn. Pick up last st with crochet hook and work ss (sl st) to finish cast-off (bind-off) round.

SCALLOPED EDGE

Round 1: *Ch 3, 1 dc (sc) into third st from hook, 1 dc (sc) into next st; rep from * thirteen times to end.

Round 2: Work 5 dc into every 3 ch space to end.

LEFT SOCK

Rounds 1–13: As Leg of Right Sock.

Round 14 (set-up round): K8, PM, k40, PM – this marker marks NEW beg of round.

Round 15: Beg of round, knit rem 8 sts from N4 with new needle, knit to end.

Round 16: Knit to last 2 sts, k2tog.

Round 17: SM, yo, k7, yo, ssk, k5, k2tog, yo, SM, [k2, k2tog, yo] to last 3 sts, k3.

Round 18 and each EVEN round: Knit.

Round 19: SM, k6, k2tog, yo, k1, yo, ssk, k6, SM, knit to end.

Round 21: SM, k5, k2tog, yo, k3, yo, ssk, k5, SM, k4, [k2tog, yo, k2] to last 3 sts, k3.

Round 23: SM, work de, k3, yo, ssk, k2, work de, SM, knit to end.

Round 25: SM, [work de, k1] twice, work de, SM, [k2, k2tog, yo] to last 3 sts, k3.

Round 27: SM, work de, k2tog, yo, k3, yo, ssk, work de, SM, knit to end.

Round 29: SM, work de, k3, yo, ssk, k2, work de, SM, k4, [k2tog, yo, k2] to last 3 sts, k3.

Round 31: SM, [work de, k1] twice, work de, SM, knit to end.

Round 33: SM, work de, k2tog, yo, k3, yo, ssk, work de, SM, [k2, k2tog, yo] to last 3 sts, k3.

Round 35: As Round 23.

Round 37: SM, [work de, k1] twice, work de, SM, k4, [k2tog, yo, k2] to last 3 sts, k3.

Round 39: As Round 27.

Round 41: SM, work de, k3, yo, ssk, k2, work de, SM, [k2, k2tog, yo] to last 3 sts, k3.

Round 43: As Round 31.

Round 45: SM, work de, k2tog, yo, k3, yo, ssk, work de, k4, [k2tog, yo, k2] to last 3 sts, k3.

Rounds 46–51: Knit.

Round 52: [K2, p2] to end.

Round 53: *K2, p2tog, yo, k2, yo, p2tog; rep from * once; **k2, p2, rep from * once; rep from ** to last 4 sts, k2, p2.

Rounds 54–63: [K2, p2] to end.

Rounds 64–65: Knit.

In next round, cast (bind) off all sts. Do NOT cut yarn. Pick up rem st with crochet hook and work ss (sl st) to finish cast-off (bind-off) round.

Finish with scalloped edge as for Right Sock.

TIES (MAKE 2)

Measure and cut 325cm (130in) length of yarn, then fold it in half. Hold the cut ends in one hand, and twist yarn at the loop. When twisted, fold it in half again, still holding the cut ends tog with the loop, and it will automatically twist again. Tie the 'loose' ends into knot. Pull the ties through eyelets and tie into bows.

DESIGNED BY

Fleur-de-Lis Slippers

These pretty fleur-de-lis slippers are knitted throughout in simple stocking (stockinette) stitch, following the charts to work the patterns.

YARN

Rowan Felted Tweed DK (50% merino wool, 25% alpaca, 25% viscose), approx.
50g (1¾oz)/175m (191yd) per ball
  One ball of Midnight 133 **(A)**
  One ball of Bilberry 151 **(B)**
  One ball of Sigh 142 **(C)**
  One ball of Pickle 155 **(D)**
  One ball of Camel 157 **(E)**
Rowan Scottish Tweed 4-ply (100% wool), approx. 25g (1oz)/110m (120yd) per ball
  One ball of Claret 013 **(G)**
  One ball of Thistle 016 **(F)**

NEEDLES

Pair of 4.00mm (US 6) knitting needles

EXTRAS

Tapestry needle

TENSION (GAUGE)

24 sts and 32 rows = 10cm (4in) square measured over St st using 4.00mm (US 6) needles.

TO FIT

One size

SKILL LEVEL

Intermediate

STRIPE SEQUENCE FOR FLEUR-DE-LIS

For the slipper upper, using Fleur-de-Lis Body chart, beg with a knit row and work in the foll colour sequence:

Rows 1–2: Using yarn B.
Rows 3–8: Using yarn B, with D for x.
Rows 9–12: Using yarn A, with D for x.
Rows 13–16: Using yarn C, with D for x.
Rows 17–18: Using yarn C, with E for x.
Rows 19–22: Using yarn C, with D for x.
Rows 23–26: Using yarn F, with D for x.
Rows 27–30: Using yarn B, with D for x.
Rows 31–34: Using yarn A, with D for x.
Rows 35–36: Using yarn A, with E for x.
Rows 37–38: Using yarn F, with E for x.
Rows 39–40: Using yarn F, with D for x.
Rows 41–44: Using yarn B, with D for x.
Rows 45–50: Using yarn A, with D for x.

SLIPPER

UPPER

Using B cast on 38 sts.
Rows 1–2: Work in St st.
Rows 3–33: Foll stripe sequence for Fleur-de-Lis pattern.

SHAPE TOE

Rows 34–49: Keeping patt correct, dec 1 st at beg of each row until 22 sts rem.

SHAPE SOLE

Foll chart for sole and heel and keep patt correct when shaping.

Rows 50–65: Using A, with B for x, inc 1 st at the beg of each row until there are 38 sts on needle.

Rows 66–122: Work straight, without shaping.

SHAPE HEEL

Rows 123–136: Keeping patt correct, dec 1 st at each end of every row until 10 sts rem.

Rows 137–151: Use yarn A, with D for x cont in patt, inc 1 st at each end of every row until 40 sts are on the needle.

Rows 152–153: Use A.

Cast (bind) off.

SLIPPER CUFF

Using E cast on 74 sts and work 1 row.

Row 2: Change to A.

Rows 3–7: Foll cuff chart, using G for x.

Row 8: Use A.

Rows 9–10: Use E.

Rows 11–19: Use A.

Cast (bind) off.

FINISHING

Fold the upper back over the sole and join the sloped side of the toe with the corresponding slopes of the sole. Repeat with the heel. Fold the cuff in half and slip stitch in place around the top of the slipper, joining the seam at the side. Sew in all loose ends.

Fleur-de-Lis Body

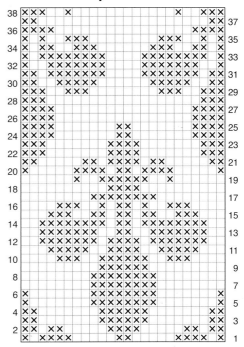

Cuff

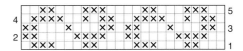

Sole and Heel

Bags

All a girl needs in life is a good bag. Take your time making these amazing knitted and crocheted bags and you'll have an accessory you can use for years and years. If you want a little clutch for going out, skip to the Golden Shell Bag with its lovely lace stitches. If you're the kind of girl who carries her life around with her, then the extra roomy Uber Bag is the one for you. Although not necessary, it's a good idea to line your bag once it's finished to make it strong enough to carry all your things.

DESIGNED BY

Chevron Holdall

Waves of bold colour turn a simple shape into an attention-grabbing bag. Crocheted in a cotton yarn that shows off stitch detail brilliantly, this bag will hold lots of kit whether you are on your way to work or out for the evening.

YARN

Rowan Handknit Cotton (100% cotton), approx. 50g (1¾oz)/ 85m (93yd) per ball

    Two balls of Decadent 314 **(A)**

    One ball of Gooseberry 219 **(B)**

    One ball of Thunder 335 **(C)**

    One ball of Linen 205 **(D)**

    One ball of Double Choc 315 **(E)**

HOOKS

One 3.50mm (E/4) crochet hook

One 4.00mm (G/6) crochet hook

EXTRAS

Tapestry needle

TENSION (GAUGE)

18 sts and 9 rows = 10cm (4in) square measured over treble (double) crochet fabric using 4.00mm (G/6) hook

MEASUREMENTS

Completed bag is 40cm (15¾ in) wide at base and 29cm (11½ in) tall.

SKILL LEVEL

Intermediate

SPECIAL ABBREVIATIONS

See page 255 for information on trtog (dctog).

SIDES (MAKE 2)

Using 3.50mm (E/4) hook and A, make 90 ch.

Row 1: 1 tr (dc) into 4th ch from hook, *1 tr (dc) into each of next 12 ch, tr3tog (dc3tog) over next 3 ch, 1 tr (dc) into each of next 12 ch**, 2 tr (dc) into each of next 2 ch; rep from * to end, ending last rep at **, 2 tr (dc) into last ch, turn. (87 sts)

Row 2: 3 ch (counts as first tr (dc)), 1 tr (dc) into tr (dc) at base of 3 ch, *1 tr (dc) into each of next 12 tr (dc), tr3tog (dc3tog) over next 3 sts, 1 tr (dc) into each of next 12 tr (dc)**, 2 tr (dc) into each of next 2 tr (dc); rep from * to end, ending last rep at **, 2 tr (dc) into top of 3 ch at beg of prev row, turn.

Row 3: 3 ch (counts as first tr (dc)), 1 tr (dc) into tr (dc) at base of 3 ch, *1 tr (dc) into each of next 11 tr (dc), tr5tog (dc5tog) over next 5 sts, 1 tr (dc) into each of next 11 tr (dc)**, 2 tr (dc) into each of next 2 tr (dc); rep from * to end, ending last rep at **, 2 tr (dc) into top of 3 ch at beg of prev row, turn. (81 sts)

Row 4: 3 ch (counts as first tr (dc)), 1 tr (dc) into tr (dc) at base of 3 ch, *1 tr (dc) into each of next 11 tr (dc), tr3tog (dc3tog) over next 3 sts, 1 tr (dc) into each of next 11 tr (dc)**, 2 tr (dc) into each of next 2 tr (dc); rep from * to end, ending last rep at **, 2 tr (dc) into top of 3 ch at beg of prev row, turn.

Cutting off and joining in colours as required, now cont in stripes as follows:

Row 5: As row 4 but with B.

Row 6: With A, 3 ch (counts as first tr (dc)), 1 tr (dc) into tr (dc) at base of 3 ch, *1 tr (dc) into each of next 10 tr (dc), tr5tog (dc5tog) over next 5 sts, 1 tr (dc) into each of next 10 tr (dc)**, 2 tr (dc) into each of next 2 tr (dc); rep from * to end, ending last rep at **, 2 tr (dc) into top of 3 ch at beg of prev row, turn. (75 sts)

Rows 7–8: With C, 3 ch (counts as first tr (dc)), 1 tr (dc) into tr (dc) at base of 3 ch, *1 tr (dc) into each of next 10 tr (dc), tr3tog (dc3tog) over next 3 sts, 1 tr (dc) into each of next 10 tr (dc)**, 2 tr (dc) into each of next 2 tr (dc); rep from * to end, ending last rep at **, 2 tr (dc) into top of 3 ch at beg of prev row, turn.

Row 9: With A, 3 ch (counts as first tr (dc)), 1 tr (dc) into tr (dc) at base of 3 ch, *1 tr (dc) into each of next 9 tr (dc), tr5tog (dc5tog) over next 5 sts, 1 tr (dc) into each of next 9 tr (dc)**, 2 tr (dc) into each of next 2 tr (dc); rep from * to end, ending last rep at **, 2 tr (dc) into top of 3 ch at beg of prev row, turn. (69 sts)

Row 10: With D, 3 ch (counts as first tr (dc)), 1 tr (dc) into tr (dc) at base of 3 ch, *1 tr (dc) into each of next 9 tr (dc), tr3tog (dc3tog) over next 3 sts, 1 tr (dc) into each of next 9 tr (dc)**, 2 tr (dc) into each of next 2 tr (dc);

rep from * to end, ending last rep at **, 2 tr (dc) into top of 3 ch at beg of prev row, turn.

Row 11: As row 10 but with B.

Row 12: With B, 3 ch (counts as first tr (dc)), 1 tr (dc) into tr (dc) at base of 3 ch, *1 tr (dc) into each of next 8 tr (dc), tr5tog (dc5tog) over next 5 sts, 1 tr (dc) into each of next 8 tr (dc)**, 2 tr (dc) into each of next 2 tr (dc); rep from * to end, ending last rep at **, 2 tr (dc) into top of 3 ch at beg of prev row, turn. (63 sts)

Row 13: With C, 3 ch (counts as first tr (dc)), 1 tr (dc) into tr (dc) at base of 3 ch, *1 tr (dc) into each of next 8 tr (dc), tr3tog (dc3tog) over next 3 sts, 1 tr (dc) into each of next 8 tr (dc)**, 2 tr (dc) into each of next 2 tr (dc); rep from * to end, ending last rep at **, 2 tr (dc) into top of 3 ch at beg of prev row, turn.

Row 14: As row 13 but with A.

Row 15: With D, 3 ch (counts as first tr (dc)), 1 tr (dc) into tr (dc) at base of 3 ch, *1 tr (dc) into each of next 7 tr (dc), tr5tog (dc5tog) over next 5 sts, 1 tr (dc) into each of next 7 tr (dc)**, 2 tr (dc) into each of next 2 tr (dc); rep from * to end, ending last rep at **, 2 tr (dc) into top of 3 ch at beg of prev row, turn. (57 sts)

Row 16: With D, 3 ch (counts as first tr (dc)), 1 tr (dc) into tr (dc) at base of 3 ch, *1 tr (dc) into each of next 7 tr (dc), tr3tog (dc3tog) over next 3 sts,

1 tr (dc) into each of next 7 tr (dc)**,
2 tr (dc) into each of next 2 tr (dc);
rep from * to end, ending last rep at **,
2 tr (dc) into top of 3 ch at beg of prev
row, turn.

Row 17: As row 16 but with B.

Row 18: With A, 3 ch (counts as first
tr (dc)), 1 tr (dc) into tr (dc) at base
of 3 ch, *1 tr (dc) into each of next
6 tr (dc), tr5tog (dc5tog) over next 5 sts,
1 tr (dc) into each of next 6 tr (dc)**,
2 tr (dc) into each of next 2 tr (dc);
rep from * to end, ending last rep at **,
2 tr (dc) into top of 3 ch at beg of prev
row, turn. (51 sts)

Row 19: With C, 3 ch (counts as first
tr (dc)), 1 tr (dc) into tr (dc) at base
of 3 ch, *1 tr (dc) into each of next
6 tr (dc), tr3tog (dc3tog) over next 3 sts,
1 tr (dc) into each of next 6 tr (dc)**,
2 tr (dc) into each of next 2 tr (dc);
rep from * to end, ending last rep at **,
2 tr (dc) into top of 3 ch at beg of prev
row, turn.

Row 20: As row 19.

Row 21: With E, 1 ch (does NOT
count as st), 1 dc (sc) into each of first
3 tr (dc), *1 htr (hdc) into each of next
3 tr (dc), 1 tr (dc) into each of next
5 sts, 1 htr (hdc) into each of next
3 tr (dc)**, 1 dc (sc) into each of next
6 tr (dc); rep from * to end, ending last
rep at **, 1 dc (sc) into each of next
2 tr (dc), 1 dc (sc) into top of 3 ch at
beg of prev row, turn.

Row 22: With E, 3 ch (counts as first
tr (dc)), miss dc (sc) at base of 3 ch,
1 tr (dc) into each of next 7 sts, 1 ch,
miss 1 st, 1 tr (dc) into each of next
33 sts, 1 ch, miss 1 st, 1 tr (dc) into
each of last 8 sts, turn.

Row 23: With E, 3 ch (counts as first
tr (dc)), miss tr (dc) at base of 3 ch,
1 tr (dc) into each tr (dc) and ch sp to
end, working last tr (dc) into top of
3 ch at beg of prev row.
Fasten off.

HANDLE

Using 4.00mm (G/6) hook and two
strands of E held together, make 151 ch.

Row 1: 1 ss (sl st) into 2nd ch from
hook, 1 ss (sl st) into each ch to end.
Fasten off.

FINISHING

Sew in all loose ends, then block and
press the pieces.
Sew Sides together along row-end and
foundation ch edges. Using photograph
as a guide, thread Handle through
'holes' of row 22 and join ends of
Handle securely.

DESIGNED BY

Fair Isle Book Bag

If you are new to Fair Isle knitting, this is a great project to start with. The sides are simple rectangles with no shaping, so you can concentrate on getting the colour patterning right without any other distractions.

YARN

Rowan Scottish Tweed 4-ply (100% wool), approx. 25g (1oz)/110m (120yd) per ball

    Four balls of Oatmeal 025 **(A)**
    One ball of Sea Green 006 **(B)**
    One ball of Porridge 024 **(C)**
    One ball of Peat 019 **(D)**
    One ball of Rust 009 **(E)**
    One ball of Gold 028 **(F)**

NEEDLES

Pair of 3.00mm (US 2) knitting needles
Pair of 3.25mm (US 3) knitting needles

EXTRAS

Nine removable stitch markers
Piece of lining fabric 80cm by 50cm (31½in by 19½in)
Piece of card (for base) 35cm by 8cm (14in by 3in)
Grosgrain ribbon (optional)
Sewing needle and thread
Tapestry needle

TENSION (GAUGE)

28 sts and 38 rows = 10cm (4in) square measured over St st using 3.25mm (US 3) needles.

MEASUREMENTS

Completed bag is 34cm (13½in) wide, 27cm (10½in) tall and 7cm (2¾in) deep.

SKILL LEVEL

Intermediate

LOVE THIS? Try knitting the Fair Isle Hat by Sue on page 102.

SIDES (MAKE 2)

Using 3.25mm (US 3) needles and A, cast on 72 sts.

Starting with a knit row, work in St st for 4 rows, ending with a WS row.

Repeating the 12-st patt rep six times across each row, work the 22 chart rows five times, then chart rows 1–14 again.

Cut off all contrast yarns and cont using A only.

Starting with a knit row, work in St st for 2 rows, ending with a WS row.

Cast (bind) off.

UPPER BORDERS (BOTH ALIKE)

Using 3.00mm (US 2) needles and A, with RS facing pick up and knit 130 sts along one row-end edge of Side piece.

Row 1: [K1, p1] to end.

Row 2: [P1, k1] to end.

These 2 rows form moss (seed) st.

Work in moss (seed) st for 4 rows more, ending with a RS row.

Cast (bind) off in moss (seed) st (on WS).

GUSSET AND STRAP

Mark centre of lower row-end edge of one Side piece.

Using 3.00mm (US 2) needles and A, cast on 20 sts.

Work in moss (seed) st as given for Upper Border until Gusset fits along lower row-end edge of Side piece from centre marker to one corner.

Place markers at both ends of last row.

Cont in moss (seed) st until Gusset, from markers, fits up cast-on or cast-off (bound-off) edge of Side piece, to cast-off (bound-off) edge of Upper Border.

Place markers at both ends of last row.

First half of Gusset completed.

Cont in moss (seed) st until Strap, from last pair of markers, measures 70cm (27½ in). Strap section completed.

Place markers at both ends of last row.

Cont in moss (seed) st until Gusset, from last pair of markers, fits down other cast-on or cast-off (bound-off) edge of Side piece to lower corner.

Place markers at both ends of last row.

Cont in moss (seed) st until Gusset, from last pair of markers, fits along lower row-end edge of Side piece from corner to centre marker. Second half of Gusset completed.

Cast (bind) off.

FINISHING

Sew in all loose ends, then block and press the pieces.

From lining fabric, cut out same size pieces as Sides and Upper Borders and gusset sections of Gusset and Strap, adding seam allowance along all edges. Join cast-on and cast-off (bound-off) ends of Gusset sections to form one long loop. Matching markers to corners of Side pieces and leaving Strap section free, sew Gusset sections to three edges of both Side pieces.

Trim card to fit neatly into base of bag and slip inside bag. Make up lining in same way as knitted pieces. Slip lining inside bag, turn under raw edges around upper opening edge and neatly sew in place.

DON'T STRETCH YOURSELF

If you are worried that the bag handle might stretch under the weight of the books you'll carry, sew a length of grosgrain ribbon to the back of it, sewing the ribbon to the lining at each end.

Key

☐ A
◉ A (P on RS, K on WS)
▨ B
☐ C
■ D
■ E
▨ F

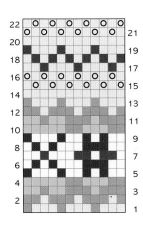

DESIGNED BY

Uber Bag

Combining the fashion for huge bags with the hot craft of crochet, this capacious tote is perfectly on trend. A variegated yarn creates intricate colour patterning with no effort and is set off by the rich chocolate handles.

YARN

Araucania Pomaire (100% pima cotton), approx. 100g (3½oz)/168m (183yd) per ball
  Three balls of multi 01 **(A)**
Rowan Handknit Cotton (100% cotton), approx. 50g (1¾ oz)/85m (93yd) per ball
  Two balls of Double Choc 315 **(B)**

HOOKS

One 3.00mm (D/3) crochet hook
One 5.00mm (H/8) crochet hook

EXTRAS

Four press studs (snap fasteners)
Piece of cotton fabric approx. 100cm by 42cm
(40in by 16½ in) to line bag (optional)
Tapestry needle

TENSION (GAUGE)

16½ sts = 10cm (4in) and 6 rows = 12.5cm (5in) measured over patt using 5.00mm (H/8) hook.

MEASUREMENTS

Completed bag is 48cm (19in) wide and 40cm (15¾ in) tall (excluding handles).

SKILL LEVEL

Advanced

SPECIAL ABBREVIATIONS

See page 255 for information on qtr (qdtr).

RIGHT SIDE PANELS (MAKE 2)

Using 5.00mm (H/8) hook and A, make 41 ch.

Row 1 (WS): 1 dc (sc) into 2nd ch from hook, 1 dc (sc) into each ch to end, turn. (40 sts)

Now work in patt as follows:

Row 2: 6 ch, insert hook into 2nd ch from hook, yoh and draw loop through, [insert hook into next ch, yoh and draw loop through] four times, insert hook into dc (sc) at base of 6 ch, yoh and draw loop through (7 loops on hook), [yoh and draw through 2 loops] six times – this forms first linked qtr (qdtr), working down side of st just made: insert hook through first loop along side of st, yoh and draw loop through, [insert hook into next loop along side of st, yoh and draw loop through] four times, insert hook into next dc (sc), yoh and draw loop through (7 loops on hook), [yoh and draw through 2 loops] six times – this forms 1 linked qtr (qdtr), 1 linked qtr (qdtr) into each dc (sc) to end, turn.

Row 3: 1 ch (does NOT count as st), 1 dc (sc) into each st to end, turn.

Last 2 rows form patt.

Work in patt for 12 rows more.

SHAPE UPPER EDGE

Row 16: 6 ch, work first 22 linked qtr (qdtr), **working down side of st just made: miss first loop along side of st, [insert hook into next loop along side of

st, yoh and draw loop through] four times, insert hook into next dc (sc), yoh and draw loop through (6 loops on hook), [yoh and draw through 2 loops] five times, working down side of st just made: miss first loop along side of st, [insert hook into next loop along side of st, yoh and draw loop through] three times, insert hook into next dc (sc), yoh and draw loop through (5 loops on hook), [yoh and draw through 2 loops] four times, working down side of st just made: miss first loop along side of st, [insert hook into next loop along side of st, yoh and draw loop through] twice, insert hook into next dc (sc), yoh and draw loop through (4 loops on hook), [yoh and draw through 2 loops] three times, working down side of st just made: miss first loop along side of st, insert hook into next loop along side of st, yoh and draw loop through, insert hook into next dc (sc), yoh and draw loop through (3 loops on hook), [yoh and draw through 2 loops] twice, 1 dc (sc) into next dc (sc), 1 ss (sl st) into next dc (sc)**, turn.

Row 17: Miss ss (sl st) at end of prev row, 1 ss (sl st) into each of next 6 sts, 1 ch (does NOT count as st), 1 dc (sc) into st at base of 1 ch (this is last linked qtr (tr tr) of prev row), 1 dc (sc) into each st to end, turn.

Row 18: 6 ch, work first 16 linked qtr (qdtr), rep from ** to ** as given for row 16, turn.

Row 19: As row 17. (16 sts)

Work in patt on these 16 sts for 2 rows more.

Fasten off.

LEFT SIDE PANELS (MAKE 2)

Work as given for Right Side Panel to start of upper edge shaping.

SHAPE UPPER EDGE

Row 16: Ss (sl st) across and into 13th st, 1 dc (sc) into next st, **1 ch, insert hook into side of dc (sc) just worked, yoh and draw loop through, insert hook into next dc (sc), yoh and draw loop through (3 loops on hook), [yoh and draw through 2 loops] twice, 1 ch, working down side of st just made: insert hook into first loop along side of st, yoh and draw loop through, insert hook into next loop along side of st, yoh and draw loop through, insert hook into next dc (sc), yoh and draw loop through (4 loops on hook), [yoh and draw through 2 loops] three times, 1 ch, working down side of st just made: insert hook into first loop along side of st, yoh and draw loop through, [insert hook into next loop along side of st, yoh and draw loop through] twice, insert hook into next dc (sc), yoh and draw loop through (5 loops on hook), [yoh and draw through 2 loops] four times, 1 ch, working down side of st just made: insert hook into first loop along side

of st, yoh and draw loop through,
[insert hook into next loop along side of
st, yoh and draw loop through] three
times, insert hook into next dc (sc), yoh
and draw loop through (6 loops on
hook), [yoh and draw through 2 loops]
five times, 1 ch, working down side of st
just made: insert hook into first loop
along side of st, yoh and draw loop
through, [insert hook into next loop
along side of st, yoh and draw loop
through] four times, insert hook into
next dc (sc), yoh and draw loop through
(7 loops on hook), [yoh and draw
through 2 loops] six times – this forms
first complete linked qtr (qdtr)**, 1 linked
qtr (qdtr) into each dc (sc) to end, turn.
Row 17: 1 ch (does NOT count as st),
1 dc (sc) into each of first 22 sts, turn.
Row 18: 1 ch (does NOT count as st),
miss first dc (sc), 1 dc (sc) into next
dc (sc), rep from ** to ** as given for
row 16, 1 linked qtr (qdtr) into each
dc (sc) to end, turn.
Row 19: 1 ch (does NOT count as st),
1 dc (sc) into each of first 16 sts, turn.
(16 sts)
Work in patt on these 16 sts for
2 rows more.
Fasten off.

HANDLES (MAKE 2)
Using 3.00mm (D/3) hook and B, make
150 ch and, taking care not to twist ch,
join with a ss (sl st) to form a ring.
Round 1: 1 ch (does NOT count as st),
1 dc (sc) into each ch to end, ss (sl st)
to first dc (sc), turn. (150 sts)
Round 2: 3 ch (counts as first tr (dc)),
miss first dc (sc), 1 tr (dc) into each of
next 8 dc (sc), 2 tr (dc) into next dc (sc),
*1 tr (dc) into each of next 9 dc (sc),
2 tr (dc) into next dc (sc); rep from * to
end, ss (sl st) to top of 3 ch at beg of
round, turn. (165 sts)
Round 3: 3 ch (counts as first tr (dc)),
miss first dc (sc), 1 tr (dc) into each of
next 9 tr (dc), 2 tr (dc) into next tr (dc),
*1 tr (dc) into each of next 10 tr (dc),
2 tr (dc) into next tr (dc); rep from * to
end, ss (sl st) to top of 3 ch at beg of
round, turn. (180 sts)
Round 4: 1 ch (does NOT count as st),
1 dc (sc) into each tr (dc) to end,
ss (sl st) to first dc (sc).
Fasten off.

FINISHING
Sew in all loose ends, then block and
press the pieces.
Joining pieces with WS together (so
seam forms a ridge on RS), sew one
Right Side Panel to one Left Side Panel
along shorter row-end edges, forming a
rectangle with a U-shaped cut-out at
top. Lay one Handle onto these pieces
so that Handle fits the U shape and sew
in place along U-shaped edge, following
the photograph.
Join other Side Panels and Handle in the
same way. Now sew Side Panels
together along longer row-end and
foundation ch edges.
At top 'corners' of Side Panels, fold
edges in to form a pleat as in
photograph. Attach a press stud (snap
fastener) to hold pleat in place.
To hold Handles together, attach press
studs (snap fasteners) approx. 10cm
(4in) above upper opening edge of
Sides.

GET IN LINE

You can line the bag with sturdy
cotton if you want; this will help
prevent the crochet fabric stretching
if you overload your giant tote. Cut
pieces of cotton fabric the same
size as the Side Panels and make
them up in the same way as the
crochet pieces. Slip lining inside
Bag, turn under raw edges around
top and neatly sew in place.

DESIGNED BY

Lace Evening Purse

A simple repeat lace pattern is given a new twist by working it in a variegated colour yarn. The changing tones of cream give a vintage feel and make the lace stitches look more complex than they really are.

YARN

Rowan Damask (57% viscose, 22% linen, 21% acrylic), approx. 50g (1¾ oz)/105m (115yd) per ball
  Two balls of Mica 040

NEEDLES

Pair of 3.75mm (US 5) knitting needles

EXTRAS

2m (2¼ yd) of 6mm (¼in) thick shiny cord
Piece of lining fabric 80cm by 30cm (31½ in by 11¾ in)
Sewing needle and thread
Tapestry needle

TENSION (GAUGE)

24 sts and 29 rows = 10cm (4in) square measured over patt using 3.75mm (US 5) needles.

MEASUREMENTS

Completed bag is 24cm (9½ in) tall, with a base diameter of 14cm (5½ in).

SKILL LEVEL

Intermediate

MAIN SECTION

Cast on 121 sts.

Row 1 (RS): P2, [k5, p2] to end.

Row 2: K2, [p5, k2] to end.

Row 3: P2, [k2tog, yfwd, k1, yfwd, skpo, p2] to end.

Row 4: As Row 2.

These 4 rows form patt.

Cont in patt until Main Section measures 24cm (9½ in) from cast-on edge, ending with a WS row.

Cast (bind) off.

BASE

Cast on 7 sts.

Work in St st as follows:

Knit 1 row.

Cast on 3 sts at beg of next 4 rows, then 2 sts at beg of foll 4 rows. (27 sts)

Inc 1 st at beg of next 3 rows. (30 sts)

Work 2 rows.

Inc 1 st at beg of next 2 rows. (32 sts)

Work 6 rows.

Dec 1 st at beg of next 2 rows. (30 sts)

Work 2 rows.

Dec 1 st at beg of next 3 rows. (27 sts)

Cast (bind) off 2 sts at beg of next 4 rows, then 3 sts at beg of foll 4 rows.

Cast (bind) off rem 7 sts.

FINISHING

Sew in all loose ends, then block and press the pieces.

From lining fabric, cut out two pieces the same size as Main Section and Base, adding seam allowance along all edges. Join row-end edges of Main Section to form a tube. Sew Base to cast-off (bound-off) edge of Main Section. Make up lining in same way. Slip lining inside Bag, turn under raw edge around upper edge and neatly sew in place. Cut a 70cm (27½ in) length of cord and tie a knot in each end approx. 9cm (3½ in) from cut ends. Unravel cut ends to form tassels. Thread this length of cord through eyelet holes of 5th patt repeat from upper edge, pull up to gather top of Bag and tie ends together loosely.

Thread remaining length of cord (this length forms handle) through eyelet rows of 4th patt repeat from upper edge at opposite side of Bag to where ends of previous length are. Knot both ends of this length of cord together approx. 12cm (4¾ in) from end and unravel cut ends of cord to form a tassel.

FINER FEELINGS

You only need a small amount of fabric for the lining and it won't take much strain, so splash out on something luxurious, like satin or soft silk. These fabrics do fray, so neaten the edges with zigzag stitch and trim excess seam allowances after making up the lining section.

DESIGNED BY

Carol Meldrum

Denim Satchel

Crisp cream denim yarn and simple crochet stitches make for a contemporary take on the classic satchel. An outer pocket closed with a strap adds practical storage as well as decorative detailing.

YARN

Rowan Denim (100% cotton), approx. 50g (1¾ oz)/93m (101yd) per ball
    Five balls of Ecru 324

HOOK

One 4.00mm (G/6) crochet hook

EXTRAS

20cm (8in) zip (zipper)
Two 4cm by 1.5cm (1½ in by ⅝ in) rectangular metal rings
Piece of card (for base) 23cm by 7cm (9in by 2¾ in)
Tapestry needle

TENSION (GAUGE)

After washing: 15 sts and 9 rows =10cm (4in) square measured over treble (double) crochet fabric using 4.00mm (G/6) hook.
Note: Rowan Denim will shrink when washed for the first time. All measurements given relate to measurements after washing.

MEASUREMENTS

Completed bag is 23cm (9in) wide, 28cm (11in) tall and 7cm (2¾in) deep.

SKILL LEVEL

Intermediate

SIDES (MAKE 2)

Make 37 ch.

Row 1: 1 tr (dc) into 4th ch from hook, 1 tr (dc) into each ch to end, turn. (35 sts)

Row 2: 3 ch (counts as first tr (dc)), miss tr (dc) at base of 3 ch, 1 tr (dc) into each tr (dc) to end, working last tr (dc) into top of 3 ch at beg of prev row, turn.

Last row forms tr (dc) fabric.

Work in tr (dc) fabric for 23 rows more.

SHAPE TOP GUSSET SECTION

Row 26: Ss (sl st) along side of last tr (dc) of prev row and down almost to base of this tr (dc), 3 ch (counts as first tr (dc)), miss tr (dc) at base of 3 ch, 1 tr (dc) around stem of next and every tr (dc) to end, working last tr (dc) around stem of 3 ch at beg of prev row, turn. (Ridge created by this row forms fold line across top of Bag.)

Row 27: 1 ch (does NOT count as st), 1 dc (sc) into each st to end, working last dc (sc) into top of 3 ch at beg of prev row.

Fasten off.

GUSSET

Make 13 ch.

Row 1: 1 tr (dc) into 4th ch from hook, 1 tr (dc) into each ch to end, turn. (11 sts)

Work in tr (dc) fabric as given for Sides for 69 rows.

Fasten off.

POCKET

Make 23 ch.

Row 1: 1 tr (dc) into 4th ch from hook, 1 tr (dc) into each ch to end, turn. (21 sts)

Work in tr (dc) fabric as given for Sides for 9 rows.

Fasten off.

POCKET FLAP

Make 23 ch.

Row 1: 1 tr (dc) into 4th ch from hook, 1 tr (dc) into each ch to end, turn. (21 sts)

Work in tr (dc) fabric as given for Sides for 7 rows.

Fasten off.

POCKET STRAP

Make 28 ch.

Row 1: 1 tr (dc) into 4th ch from hook, 1 tr (dc) into each ch to end, turn. (26 sts)

Work in tr (dc) fabric as given for Sides for 2 rows.

Fasten off.

POCKET TAB

Make 23 ch.

Row 1: 1 tr (dc) into 4th ch from hook, 1 tr (dc) into each ch to end. (11 sts)

Fasten off.

STRAP

Make 143 ch.

Row 1: 1 tr (dc) into 4th ch from hook, 1 tr (dc) into each ch to end, turn. (141 sts)

Work in tr (dc) fabric as given for Sides for 2 rows.

Fasten off.

FINISHING

Sew in all loose ends. Do NOT press. Machine hot-wash all pieces (and small ball of yarn for seaming) following ball-band instructions to shrink them to correct size. Once dry, block and press.

Using photograph as a guide, sew Pocket centrally onto one Side piece – position lower edge of Pocket 5 rows up from foundation ch edge. Sew Pocket Strap onto Pocket Flap as in photograph – one end of Strap will extend beyond lower edge of Flap. Sew Flap to Side above Pocket. Sew Pocket Tab onto Pocket to correspond with end of Strap. Insert zip (zipper) between upper (last row) edges of Sides.

Mark centre point of row-end edges of Gusset. With WS together (so seams form a ridge on RS), and matching this centre point to centre point of foundation ch edge of Sides, sew Gusset to foundation ch and row-end edges of Sides, stopping level with ridge row – Gusset should extend beyond ridge row for approx. 2 rows. Thread metal rings onto these extensions, fold over ends of Gusset and securely sew in place, attaching row-end edges of top gusset sections at same time.

Thread ends of Strap onto rings, fold under 4cm (1½ in) and sew in place. At base of Bag, fold gusset level with corners and sew across Gusset to form a ridge (to match other seams). Slip card inside Bag and secure to base section.

DESIGNED BY

Fair Isle Tote

Zesty, contemporary colours bring traditional Fair Isle right into the 21st century and make this bag a modern classic. The rib top and looping straps add understated detailing that complements the design.

YARN

Rowan Pure Wool DK (100% superwash wool), approx. 50g (1¾ oz)/125m (137yd) per ball

Three balls of Hay 014 **(A)**
One ball of Barley 015 **(B)**
One ball of Avocado 019 **(C)**
One ball of Shale 002 **(D)**
One ball of Damson 030 **(E)**
One ball of Kiss 036 **(F)**
One ball of Glade 021 **(G)**

NEEDLES

Pair of 3.25mm (US 3) knitting needles
Pair of 4.00mm (US 6) knitting needles

EXTRAS (OPTIONAL)

Piece of fabric approx. 65cm by 37cm (25½in by 14½in) for lining
Sewing needle and thread
Tapestry needle

TENSION (GAUGE)

24 sts and 32 rows = 10cm (4in) square measured over patt using 4.00mm (US 6) needles.

MEASUREMENTS

Completed bag is 30cm (11¾in) wide and 36cm (14in) tall.

SKILL LEVEL

Intermediate

LOVE THIS? Try knitting the Fair Isle Beret by Fiona on page 74.

SIDES (MAKE 2)

Using 4.00mm (US 6) needles and A,
cast on 73 sts.

Starting with a knit row, repeating the
8-st patt rep nine times across rows and
working edge st as indicated, work in
St st from chart as follows:

Work all 30 rows of chart three times,
then chart rows 1–4 again, inc 1 st at
centre of last row and ending with a
WS row. (74 sts)

Cut off contrast yarns and cont with
A only.

Change to 3.25mm (US 3) needles.

Next row (RS): K2, [p2, k2] to end.

Next row: P2, [k2, p2] to end.

Work in rib as set for 6 rows more,
ending with a WS row.

Next row (RS): Rib 12, cast (bind)
off 2 sts (to form eyelet hole for Strap),
rib to last 14 sts, cast (bind) off 2 sts
(to form other eyelet hole for Strap), rib
to end.

Next row: Rib to end, casting on
2 sts over those cast (bound) off on
previous row.

Work in rib for 8 rows more, ending with
a WS row.

Cast (bind) off in rib.

STRAPS (MAKE 2)

Using 3.25mm (US 3) needles and A,
cast on 6 sts.

Starting with a knit row, work in St st
until Strap measures 128cm (50½ in),
ending with a WS row.

Cast (bind) off.

FINISHING

Sew in all loose ends, then block and
press the pieces.

Join the Sides along cast-on and row-
end edges.

Starting on RS of work, take one end of
one Strap through one eyelet hole on
one side, then take other end of same
Strap through other eyelet hole of same
Side. Join ends of Strap. Thread ends
of other Strap through eyelet holes of
other Side and join ends in same way.
(Straps will roll in on themselves to form
soft tubes.)

If you are lining the bag, cut two pieces
the same size as Sides, adding seam
allowance along all edges except the top
edge. Sew the two lining pieces together
along side and lower edges, leaving
upper (opening) edge open.

Slip lining inside Bag, turn under raw
edge around upper edge so that it lies
just below the ribbed top of the knitted
bag and neatly sew in place.

Key

- ☐ A
- ▨ B
- ☐ C
- ▨ D
- ■ E
- ■ F
- ■ G

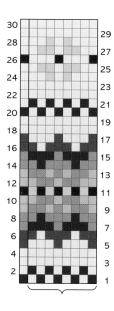

DESIGNED BY

LOVE THIS? Try knitting the Elizabethan Beret by Sue on page 78.

Black and White Evening Bag

Whether you are going to a smart wedding, a classy cocktail party or on a special night out with the girls, this little bag is the perfect accessory. It's quick to knit and you can choose colours and trims to match your outfit.

YARN

Rowan Cashcotton DK (35% cotton, 25% polyamide, 18% angora, 13% viscose, 9% cashmere), approx. 50g (1¾oz)/ 130m (142yd) per ball
    One ball of White 600 **(A)**
    One ball of Black 607 **(B)**

NEEDLES

Pair of 3.25mm (US 3) knitting needles
Pair of 4.00mm (US 6) knitting needles
One 3.25mm (D/3) crochet hook

EXTRAS

Five different fancy black buttons – four 20mm (¾in) diameter buttons for handles and one 15mm (⅝in) diameter button for flower centre
90cm (1yd) of 5cm (2in) wide black lace
Eleven black sequins
Piece of lining fabric approx. 45cm by 30cm (17¾in by 11¾in)
Sewing needle and thread
Tapestry needle

TENSION (GAUGE)

22 sts and 30 rows = 10cm (4in) square measured over St st using 4.00mm (US 6) needles.

MEASUREMENTS

Completed bag is 20cm (8in) wide and 24cm (9½in) tall.

SKILL LEVEL

Intermediate

MAIN SECTION

Using 3.25mm (US 3) needles and B, cast on 88 sts.

Row 1 (RS): [K1, p1] to end.

Row 2: [P1, k1] to end.

These 2 rows form moss (seed) st.

Work in moss (seed) st for 6 rows more, ending with a WS row.

Cut off B and join in A.

Change to 4.00mm (US 6) needles. Starting with a knit row, work in St st until Main Section measures 24cm (9½ in) from cast-on edge, ending with a RS row.

Cast (bind) off.

HANDLES (MAKE 2)

Using 3.25mm (US 3) needles and B, cast on 8 sts.

Work in moss (seed) st as given for Main Section for 30cm (11¾ in), ending with a RS row.

Cast (bind) off.

FLOWER

Using 3.25mm (D/3) crochet hook and A, make 6 ch and join with ss (sl st) to form a ring.

Round 1: 1 ch (does NOT count as st), 1 dc (sc) into ring, [1 tr (dc), 1 dtr (tr), 4 ch and 1 dc (sc) into ring] six times, replacing dc (sc) at end of last rep with ss (sl st) to first dc (sc). (6 petals)

Round 2: [4 ch (keeping this ch behind petals of prev round), 1 ss (sl st) into next dc (sc)] six times, working last ss (sl st) into same place as ss (sl st) at end of prev round.

Round 3: 1 ch (does NOT count as st), [1 dc (sc), 1 tr (dc), 1 dtr (tr), 4 ch, 1 dc (sc), 1 tr (dc), 1 dtr (tr), 4 ch and 1 dc (sc)] into each ch sp to end, ss (sl st) to first dc (sc). (12 petals)

Round 4: [5 ch (keeping this ch behind petals of prev round), miss 1 dc (sc), 1 ss (sl st) into next dc (sc)] six times, working last ss (sl st) into same place as ss (sl st) at end of prev round.

Round 5: 1 ch (does NOT count as st), [1 dc (sc), 8 ch, 1 dc (sc) and 8 ch] into each ch sp to last ch sp, 1 dc (sc) into last ch sp, 4 ch, 1 tr (dc) into first dc (sc). (11 ch sps)

Round 6: 3 ch (counts as first tr (dc)), 1 tr (dc) into ch sp partly formed by tr (dc) at end of prev round, *4 ch**, [2 tr (dc), 2 ch and 2 tr (dc)] into next ch sp; rep from* to end, ending last rep at **, 2 tr (dc) into same ch sp used at beg of round, 2 ch, ss (sl st) to top of 3 ch at beg of round.

Round 7: 1 ch (does NOT count as st), 1 dc (sc) into st at base of 1 ch, 1 dc (sc) into next tr (dc), *[2 dc (sc), 6 ch and 2 dc (sc)] into next ch sp, 1 dc (sc) into each of next 2 tr (dc), 2 dc (sc) into next ch sp**, 1 dc (sc) into each of next 2 tr (dc); rep from * to end, ending last rep at **, ss (sl st) to first dc (sc).
Fasten off.

FINISHING

Sew in all loose ends, then block and press the knitted pieces.

From lining fabric, cut out same size piece as Main Section, adding seam allowance along all edges.

Cut lace into two equal lengths. Using photograph as a guide, sew lace across knitted Main Section – one strip just below moss (seed) st section and other strip just above cast-off (bound-off) edge. Fold Main Section in half and sew side (row-end edge) and base (cast-off (bound-off) edge) seam.

Sew Handles to each side around upper edge so that ends of Handles are on RS of moss (seed) st upper band, positioning Handles approx. 7.5cm (3in) apart. Sew one of the larger buttons onto each Handle end.

Sew Flower onto one side of Bag as in photograph, attaching the smaller button at the centre. Sew a sequin onto each group of 4 tr (dc) around Flower.

Make up lining in same way as Main Section. Slip lining inside Bag, turn under raw edge around upper opening edge and neatly slip stitch in place.

GRIDLOCK

To attach the lace pieces, first pin them in position. Use the grid formed by the stitches and rows of the knitted fabric to make sure that the pieces are straight. Use a sewing thread that matches the lace, not the yarn, and a fine hand-sewing needle. Make tiny slip stitches, going just over the edge of the lace, then through the knitted fabric. Follow the shaped edge of the lace accurately, being careful not to pull it out of shape. If the shaped edge is quite fancy, you may find it easier to quickly tack (baste) it in place first before slip stitching it.

LOVE THIS? Try knitting the Inca Hat by Fiona on page 97.

DESIGNED BY

Inca Satchel

Taking inspiration from traditional designs, but working them in today's colour palette, this satchel-style bag uses both intarsia and Fair Isle techniques, so it's a must for lovers of colour knitting.

YARN

Rowan Baby Alpaca DK (100% baby alpaca), approx. 50g (1¾oz)/100m (109yd) per ball

Four balls of Jacob 205 **(A)**
Two balls of Lincoln 209 **(B)**
One ball of Southdown 208 **(C)**

NEEDLES

Pair of 3.25mm (US 3) knitting needles
Pair of 3.75mm (US 5) knitting needles

EXTRAS

Three 15mm (⅝ in) diameter buttons
Tapestry needle

TENSION (GAUGE)

24 sts and 36 rows = 10cm (4in) square measured over patt using 3.75mm (US 5) needles.

MEASUREMENTS

Completed bag is 30cm (11¾ in) wide, 22cm (8½ in) tall and 5cm (2in) deep.

SKILL LEVEL

Advanced

BACK AND FRONT (BOTH ALIKE)

Using 3.75mm (US 5) needles and A, cast on 71 sts.

Knit 2 rows, ending with a WS row.

Cutting off and joining in colours as required, stranding yarn not in use loosely across WS of work, reading odd-numbered rows as knit rows from right to left and even-numbered rows as purl rows from left to right, now work in patt from chart A as follows:

Row 3 (RS): With A k3, work edge st of chart, then rep the 8-st patt rep eight times, with A k3.

Row 4: With A k3, rep the 8-st patt rep eight times, work edge st, with A k3.

These 2 rows set the sts – central 65 sts in Fair Isle patt from chart with 3 sts at each end of every row in garter st with A.

Keeping sts correct as set and working appropriate rows of chart, work chart rows 3–34, then chart rows 1–34 again, ending with a WS row.

Cut off contrast yarns and cont with A only.

Change to 3.25mm (US 3) needles.

Knit 6 rows, ending with a WS row.

Cast (bind) off.

FLAP

Using 3.25mm (US 3) needles and A, cast on 70 sts.

Knit 2 rows, ending with a WS row.

Row 3 (RS): K5, *cast (bind) off 2 sts (to make a buttonhole), k until there are 27 sts on RH needle after cast-off (bind-off); rep from * once more, cast (bind) off 2 sts (to make third buttonhole), k to end.

Row 4: Knit to end, casting on 2 sts over those cast (bound) off on previous row. Work in garter st for 2 rows more, ending with a WS row.

Change to 3.75mm (US 5) needles.

Row 7 (RS): Knit.

Row 8: K3, p to last 3 sts, k3.

Rows 9–10: As Rows 7–8.

Joining in and cutting off B as required, stranding yarn not in use loosely across WS of work, reading odd-numbered rows as knit rows from right to left and even-numbered rows as purl rows from left to right, now work in patt from chart B as follows:

Row 11 (RS): With A k3, work next 64 sts as row 1 of chart B, with A k3.

Row 12: With A k3, work next 64 sts as row 2 of chart B, with A k3.

These 2 rows set the sts – central 64 sts in Fair Isle patt from chart with 3 sts at each end of every row in garter st with A.

Keeping sts correct as set and working appropriate rows of chart, work chart rows 3–30, ending with a WS row.

Cut off B and cont with A only.

Rep Rows 7–8 until Flap measures 22cm (8½in), ending with a WS row.

Cast (bind) off.

BASE

Using 3.75mm (US 5) needles and A, cast on 13 sts.

Row 1 (RS): Knit.

Row 2: K2, p9, k2.

Using a separate ball of yarn for each block of colour and twisting yarns together on WS where they meet to avoid holes forming, cont as follows:

Row 3: With A k6, with B k1, with A k6.

Row 4: With A k2, p3, with B p3, with A p3, k2.

Row 5: With A k4, with B k5, with A k4.

Row 6: With A k2, p1, with B p7, with A p1, k2.

Row 7: With A k3, with B k7, with A k3.

Row 8: With A k2, p2, with B p2, with A p1, with B p2, with A p2, k2.

These 8 rows form the patt.

Cont in patt for 82 rows more, ending after patt row 2 and with a WS row.

Cast (bind) off.

SIDE GUSSETS (MAKE 2)

Using 3.75mm (US 5) needles and A, cast on 13 sts.

Starting with patt row 1, work in patt as given for Base for 66 rows, ending after patt row 2 and with a WS row.

Cast (bind) off.

STRAP

Using 3.75mm (US 5) needles and A, cast on 13 sts.

Starting with patt row 1, work in patt as given for Base until Strap measures

approx. 142cm (56in), ending after patt row 2 and with a WS row.

Cast (bind) off.

Chart A

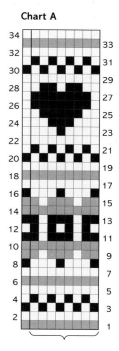

Key

☐ A

■ B

▨ C

FINISHING

Sew in all loose ends, then block and
press the pieces.
Matching cast-off (bound-off) and
cast-on edges, sew row-end edges of
Gussets to row-end edges of Back
and Front. Sew Base to cast on edges
of Back, Front and Gussets. Sew
cast-off (bound–off) edge of Flap to
cast-off (bound–off) edge of Back. Sew
cast-on and cast-off (bound–off) ends of
Strap to cast-off (bound–off) edges of
Gussets. Sew buttons onto Front to
correspond with buttonholes in Flap.

DARN IT!

If you prefer, you can Swiss darn
the reindeers' antlers after you have
finished the knitting. Many knitters
find it tricky to work single stitches
neatly in intarsia and Swiss darning
them is a good alternative.
This bag would also look great
knitted in strong colours: try a deep
pink background with lime green
and aqua Fair Isle for a completely
different effect.

Chart B

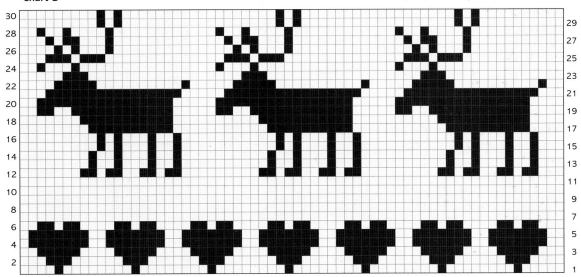

DESIGNED BY

Sue Bradley

Duffle Bag

This bag might look intricate, but it's just simple stripes worked in a double rib stitch, so all you need to do is knit and purl – easy!

YARN

Rowan Pure Wool Aran (100% superwash wool), approx. 100g (3½ oz)/170m (186yd) per ball

One ball of Ivory 670 **(A)**

One ball of Cedar 670 **(B)**

One ball of Paper 671 **(C)**

NEEDLES

Pair of 5.00mm (US 8) knitting needles

EXTRAS

Four 15mm (⅝in) diameter buttons

Tapestry needle

TENSION (GAUGE)

24 sts and 28 rows = 10cm (4in) square measured over patt using 5.00mm (US 8) needles.

MEASUREMENTS

Completed bag is 40cm (15¾in) tall, with a base diameter of 20cm (8in).

SKILL LEVEL

Beginner

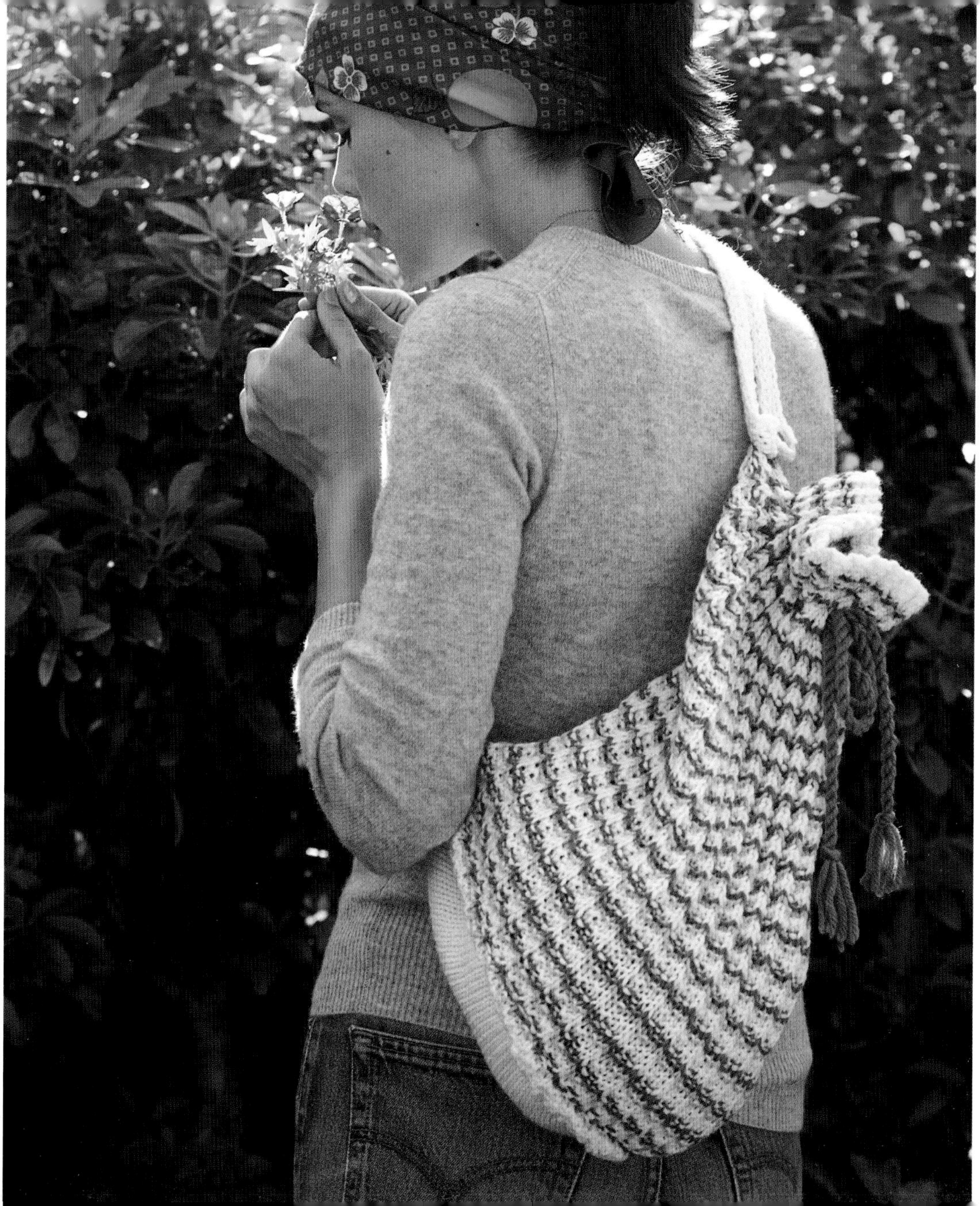

MAIN SECTION

With A, cast on 123 sts.

Row 1 (RS): K2, [p2, k2] to last st, p1.

Row 2: As Row 1.

These 2 rows form stitch patt.

Work in patt for 2 rows more, ending with a WS row.

Keeping patt correct, now work in stripes as follows:

Row 5: With B.

Row 6: With C.

Rows 7–9: With A.

Last 5 rows form stripe sequence.

Cont in patt in stripe sequence as set for 8 rows more, ending with a RS row.

Next row (eyelet row) (WS): With A, k2, [p2tog, yo, k2] to end.

Cont in patt in stripe sequence as set until Main Section measures approx. 40cm (15¾ in) from cast-on edge, ending after 3 rows with A.

With A, work in patt for 1 row more.

Cast (bind) off.

BASE

With A, cast on 14 sts.

Knit 1 row (RS).

Inc 1 st at each end of next 14 rows (40 sts).

Work 21 rows in St st, ending with a WS row.

Dec 1 st at each end of next 14 rows, ending with a WS row.

Cast (bind) off rem 14 sts.

STRAPS (MAKE 2)

With A, cast on 8 sts.

Row 1: [K2, p2] twice.

Rep this row until Strap measures 50cm (19½ in).

Cast (bind) off.

FINISHING

Sew in all loose ends. Do NOT press. Join row-end edges of Main Section to form a tube. Sew Base to cast-off (bound-off) edge of Main Section, then fold along seam and stitch through both layers to accentuate base seam.

With B, make a twisted cord approx. 90cm (1yd) long and knot ends, leaving little tassels. Thread twisted cord through eyelet row and tie ends in a bow to close bag.

Using photograph as a guide, attach Straps near eyelet row and to base seam by securely sewing a button through end of Strap and Main Section.

COLOURFUL CARRY-ALL

Although each colour of yarn is used to make a single-row stripe or a three-row stripe, the stripe sequence has been designed so that the colour you need next will always be at the right end of a row when you need it. However, to keep the yarns to hand and prevent untidy loops forming along the edge of the knitting, you need to carry the yarns not in use up the side of the work. This is easy: when you get to the end of a row, swap to the new colour of yarn needed and, before you start working the row, loop this yarn around the yarns not being used to hold them against the edge of the knitting. Do this at the end of every row and your edges will be tidy and the yarn you need next will always be just there, ready to go. Don't pull the yarns being carried too tight or you will tighten the edge of the knitting.

DESIGNED BY

Jacobean Tote

Exotic flowers in jewel colours and clever handle detailing make this bag something special. The main panels have no shaping, so there is just the colour knitting to concentrate on.

YARN

Rowan Pure Wool DK (100% superwash wool), approx. 50g (1¾oz)/125m (137yd) per ball

Four balls of Hay 014 **(A)**

Small amounts of same yarn in the following colours for intarsia pattern:

Pomegranate 029 **(B)**, Gilt 032 **(C)**, Hessian 016 **(D)**, Cypress 007 **(E)**, Indigo 010 **(F)**, Damson 030 **(G)**, Parsley 020 **(H)**, Shamrock 023 **(I)** and Spice 034 **(J)**

NEEDLES

Pair of 3.25mm (US 3) knitting needles
Pair of 4.00mm (US 6) knitting needles

EXTRAS

Tapestry needle

TENSION (GAUGE)

22 sts and 30 rows = 10cm (4in) square measured over St st using 4.00mm (US 6) needles.

MEASUREMENTS

Completed bag is 41cm (16in) wide and 33cm (13in) tall.

SKILL LEVEL

Advanced

SIDES (MAKE 2)

Using 4.00mm (US 6) needles and A, cast on 90 sts.

Starting with a knit row, work in St st from chart until all 90 rows of chart have been completed, ending with a WS row.

Cut off contrast yarns and cont with A only.

Change to 3.25mm (US 3) needles.

Knit 22 rows, ending with a WS row.

Cast (bind) off.

BASE

Using 4.00mm (US 6) needles and A, cast on 70 sts.

Knit 1 row.

Row 2 (WS): Cast on 3 sts, p to end.

Row 3: Cast on 3 sts, k to end.

Rep Rows 2–3 twice. (88 sts).

Work 6 rows in St st, ending with a RS row.

Row 14: Cast (bind) off 3 sts, p to end.

Row 15: Cast (bind) off 3 sts, k to end.

Rep Rows 14–15 twice more.

Cast (bind) off rem 70 sts.

HANDLES (MAKE 2)

Using 3.25mm (US 3) needles and A, cast on 11 sts.

Row 1 (RS): Knit.

Row 2: K1, p9, k1.

Rep these 2 rows until Handle measures 116cm (45½ in), ending with a WS row.

Cast (bind) off.

COLOURING IN

The flower shapes should be worked using the intarsia technique, but the detailing within them is best done using the Fair Isle technique. For intarsia instructions, turn to page 248; for Fair Isle, turn to page 249.

You can work the flower pattern on one side of the bag only and just knit the other side in plain cream if you prefer. You may need an extra ball of the cream yarn to do this.

HANDLE LOOPS (MAKE 4)

Using 3.25mm (US 3) needles and A, cast on 11 sts.

Row 1 (RS): Knit.

Row 2: K1, p9, k1.

Rep these 2 rows until Handle Loop measures 10cm (4in), ending with a WS row.

Cast (bind) off.

FINISHING

Embroider stem stitch curls onto Sides as shown on chart.

Sew in all loose ends, then block and press the pieces.

Join sides along row-end edges. Sew Base to cast-on edges of Sides, matching side seams to centre of Base

---

Key

☐	A
■	B
☐	C
■	D
■	E
■	F
■	G
■	H
■	I
■	J

---

row-end edges. Around upper opening edge, fold garter st section in half to inside and slip stitch in place.

Join row-end edges of Handle Loops, to form four short tubes. Using photograph as a guide, sew ends of Handle Loops inside upper edge of Bag, positioning Loops approx. 4cm (1½ in) in from side seams.

Join row-end edges of Handles, to form two long tubes. Starting on RS of work, take one end of one Handle through one Handle Loop on one side, then take other end of same Handle through other Handle Loop of same Side. Join ends of Handle. Thread ends of other Handle through Handle Loops of other Side and join ends in same way.

DESIGNED BY

Golden Shell Bag

Unashamedly feminine, this delicate bag has a knitted lining as well as a lace knit outer, so it's as practical as it is pretty. Pearls decorate this version, but you could use crystal beads that tone with your dress.

YARN

Louisa Harding Glisten (97% nylon, 3% polyester), approx. 50g (1¾oz)/85m (93yd) per ball
  One ball of gold 4 **(A)**
Louisa Harding Nautical Cotton (100% mercerised cotton), approx. 50g (1¾oz)/85m (93yd) per ball
  One ball of black 15 **(B)**

NEEDLES

Pair of 3.75mm (US 5) knitting needles
Pair of 4.50mm (US 7) knitting needles
One 3.00mm (D/3) crochet hook

EXTRAS

Small amount of waste yarn (for cast-on edges)
10cm (4in) zipper
Three pearl beads
Two removable stitch markers (or use short lengths of waste yarn)
Sewing needle and strong thread
Tapestry needle

TENSION (GAUGE)

20 sts and 29 rows = 10cm (4in) square measured over patt using 4.50mm (US 7) needles and A.
20 sts and 28 rows = 10cm (4in) square measured over St st using 4.50mm (US 7) needles and B.

MEASUREMENTS

Completed bag is 22cm (8½ in) wide (at widest point) and 15cm (6in) tall.

SKILL LEVEL

Advanced

SPECIAL ABBREVIATIONS

See page 255 for information on three-needle cast (bind) off.

OUTER SECTION

Using 4.50mm (US 7) needles and waste yarn, cast on 26 sts.

Purl 1 row.

Cut off waste yarn and join in A.

Row 1 (RS): Knit.

Now work in patt as follows:

Row 2 (WS): K1, [yfwd, k2tog] to last st, k1.

Row 3: P1, [yrn, p2tog] to last st, p1.

Row 4: As row 2.

Row 5: Slip first st purlwise with yarn at front (RS) of work, then take yarn to back (WS) of work (thereby twisting slipped st), m1, knit to end. (27 sts)

Row 6: Purl.

Row 7: Slip first st purlwise with yarn at front (RS) of work, then take yarn to back (WS) of work, m1, k17, wrap next st (by bringing yarn to front of work, slipping next st from LH needle onto RH needle, taking yarn to back of work and then slipping same st back onto LH needle – when working back across wrapped sts, work the wrapped st and the wrapping loop together as though they were one st) and turn.

Row 8: Purl.

Row 9: Slip first st purlwise with yarn at front (RS) of work, then take yarn to back (WS) of work, m1, k9, wrap next st and turn.

Row 10: Purl.

Row 11: Slip first st purlwise with yarn at front (RS) of work, then take yarn to back (WS) of work, k to end. (29 sts)

Row 12: Purl.

Row 13: Slip first st purlwise with yarn at front (RS) of work, then take yarn to back (WS) of work, k2tog, k8, wrap next st and turn.

Row 14: Purl.

Row 15: Slip first st purlwise with yarn at front (RS) of work, then take yarn to back (WS) of work, k2tog, k16, wrap next st and turn.

Row 16: Purl.

Row 17: Slip first st purlwise with yarn at front (RS) of work, then take yarn to back (WS) of work, k2tog, k to end. (27 sts)

Last 16 rows form patt.

Rows 18–65: Rep Rows 2–17 three times.

Rows 66–68: As Rows 2–4.

Row 69: Knit.

Row 70 (WS): Knit (to form fold line for side of Bag).

Place marker at upper (straight) edge of last row.

Row 71: Knit.

Rows 72–135: Rep Rows 2–17 four times.

Rows 136–138: As Rows 2–4.

Row 139: Knit.

Row 140 (WS): Knit (to form fold line for other side of Bag).

Place marker at upper (straight) edge of last row.

Slip sts of first row in A onto a spare needle, carefully unravelling waste yarn. Fold Main Section in half with RS together and cast (bind) off both sets of sts (those of row 140 and those just slipped onto spare needle) together by taking 1 st from first needle together with corresponding st from other needle.

OUTER UPPER BORDERS (BOTH ALIKE)

Using 3.75mm (US 5) needles and A, with RS facing pick up and knit 36 sts along first part of straight row-end edge of Outer Section between markers at ends of fold lines.

Row 1 (WS): K1, [yfwd, k2tog] to last st, k1.

Row 2: P1, [yrn, p2tog] to last st, p1.

Row 3: As row 1.

Rows 4–5: Knit.

Cast (bind) off.

Work second Upper Border in exactly the same way but do NOT fasten off last cast-off (bound-off) st.

Slip this last loop onto 3.00mm (D/3) crochet hook and make a ch 25cm (10in) long, work a ss (sl st) into first cast-off (bound-off) st of other Upper Border and fasten off.

INNER SECTION

Using 4.50mm (US 7) needles and waste yarn, cast on 24 sts.

Purl 1 row.

Cut off waste yarn and join in B.

Row 1 (RS): Knit.

Now work in patt as follows:

Row 2 (WS): Purl.

Row 3: Knit.

Row 4: Purl.

Row 5: Sl1, m1, k to end (25 sts).

Row 6: Purl.

Row 7: Sl1, m1, k15, wrap next st and turn.

Row 8: Purl.

Row 9: Sl1, m1, k7, wrap next st and turn.

Row 10: Purl.

Row 11: Sl1, k to end (27 sts).

Row 12: Purl.

Row 13: Sl1, k2tog, k6, wrap next st and turn.

Row 14: Purl.

Row 15: Sl1, k2tog, k14, wrap next st and turn.

Row 16: Purl.

Row 17: Slip first st purlwise with yarn at front (RS) of work, then take yarn to back (WS) of work, k2tog, k to end. (24 sts)

Last 16 rows form patt.

Rows 18–65: Rep Rows 2–17 three times.

Rows 66–68: As Rows 2–4.

Row 69 (WS): Knit (to form fold line for side of Bag).

Place marker at straight edge of last row.

Rows 70–133: As Rows 2–17, four times.

Rows 134–136: As Rows 2–4.

Slip sts of first row in B onto a spare needle, carefully unravelling waste yarn. Fold Inner Section in half with RS together and cast (bind) off both sets of sts (those of row 136 and those just slipped onto spare needle) together by taking 1 st from first needle together with corresponding st from other needle.

INNER UPPER BORDERS (BOTH ALIKE)

Using 3.75mm (US 5) needles and B, with WS facing pick up and knit 32 sts along first part of straight row-end edge of Inner Section between marker and seam.

Row 1: Purl.

Cast (bind) off.

Work second Upper Border in exactly the same way.

FINISHING

Sew in all loose ends, then block and press the pieces.

Sew shaped base seam of Outer Section, then sew shaped base seam of Inner Section.

Insert zipper into opening edge of Inner Section. Slip Inner Section inside Outer Section and sew together around upper edge, stitching along pick-up row of Outer Upper Borders.

Thread beads onto strong sewing thread and attach to zip (zipper) pull as in photograph.

DESIGNED BY

Stripy Bag

Self-striping yarn is marvellous stuff, allowing you to concentrate on shaping and stitch detail while the colour patterning takes care of itself. This big bag makes the most of the yarn with varying-width stripes on different sections.

YARN

Twilley's Freedom Spirit (100% pure new wool), approx. 50g (1¾oz)/120m (131yd) per ball

Six balls of Essence 507 **(A)**

Twilley's Freedom Wool (100% pure new wool), approx. 50g (1¾oz)/50m (54yd) per ball

Two balls of Navy 423 **(B)**

NEEDLES

Pair of 4.00mm (US 6) knitting needles

Pair of 6.50mm (US 10½) knitting needles

Two 6.50mm (US 10½) double-pointed needles (dpns)

EXTRAS

Two cable needles

30cm (12in) zipper

Piece of buckram 12cm by 52cm (4¾in by 20½in)

Sewing needle and thread

Sixteen removable stitch markers (or use short lengths of waste yarn)

Tapestry needle

TENSION (GAUGE)

22 sts and 28 rows = 10cm (4in) square measured over St st using 4.00mm (US 6) needles and A.

25 sts and 34 rows = 10cm (4in) square measured over patt using 6.50mm (US 10½) needles and A.

MEASUREMENTS

Completed bag is 46cm (18in) wide, 25cm (10in) tall (excluding strap) and 12cm (4¾ in) deep.

SKILL LEVEL

Advanced

SIDES (MAKE 2)

Using 4.00mm (US 6) needles and A, cast on 86 sts.

Place markers at both ends of cast-on edge.

Starting with a knit row, cont in St st as follows:

Inc 1 st at each end of next 7 rows, then on foll 4th row. (102 sts)

Place markers at both ends of last row.

Work 75 rows, ending with a WS row.

Next row (RS): K13, *slip next 3 sts onto a cable needle, then foll 3 sts onto second cable needle, fold work so that cable needles and LH needle form a 'Z' shape, knit tog first st from first cable needle with last st from second cable needle and first st from LH needle, knit tog centre sts from both cable needles with next st from LH needle, knit tog last st from first cable needle with first st from second cable needle and next st from LH needle – first half of pleat completed, slip next 3 sts onto a cable needle, then foll 3 sts onto second cable needle, fold work so that cable needles and LH needle form an 'S' shape, knit tog first st from LH needle with last st from second cable needle and first st from first cable needle, knit tog next st from LH needle with centre sts from both cable needles, knit tog next st from LH needle with first st from second cable needle and last st from first cable needle – second half of pleat completed*, k11, rep from * to * once

more – second pleat completed, k11, rep from * to * once more – third pleat completed, k13. (66 sts)

Place markers at both ends of last row.

SHAPE TOP GUSSET

Change to 6.50mm (US 10½) needles. Now work in patt as follows:

Row 1 (WS): *P1, take yarn to back (RS) of work, slip next st purlwise, bring yarn to front (WS) of work; rep from * to end.

Row 2: *K1, bring yarn to front (RS) of work, slip next st purlwise, take yarn to back (WS) of work; rep from * to end.

These 2 rows form patt.

Work in patt for 8 rows more, ending with a RS row.

Change to 4.00mm (US 6) needles.

Row 11 (WS): With RH needle, pick up loop of first st of last marked row and place on LH needle, p this loop tog with first st on LH needle (forming small ridge on RS of work), *pick up loop of next st of marked row and place on LH needle, p this loop tog with next st on LH needle; rep from * to end.

Change to 6.50mm (US 10½) needles. Starting with row 2, work in patt for 12 rows, ending with a WS row.

Cast (bind) off.

COOL IN THE SHADE

This bag would also look fabulous knitted in different shades of one plain colour. Try using one shade for the sides, a second for the gusset and strap section and a third shade for the piping.

GUSSET AND STRAP

Using 6.50mm (US 10½) needles and A, cast on 30 sts.

Starting with row 2, work in patt as given for top gusset for 68 rows, ending with a WS row.

Place markers at both ends of last row – these markers match markers at ends of cast-on edge of Sides.

Work 20 rows.

Place markers at both ends of last row – these markers match markers at top of shaped row-end edges of Sides.

Work 28 rows, ending with a WS row.

Keeping patt correct, dec 1 st at each end of next and 2 foll 28th rows. (24 sts)

Work 9 rows.

Place markers at both ends of last row – these markers match to ridges of Sides at start of top gusset.

Work 18 rows, ending with a WS row.

Keeping patt correct, dec 1 st at each end of next and every foll 28th row until 14 sts rem.

Work 63 rows.

Inc 1 st at each end of next and every foll 28th row until there are 24 sts, taking inc sts into patt.
Work 17 rows.
Place markers at both ends of last row – last section forms strap and these markers match to other end of ridges of Sides at start of top gusset.
Work 10 rows.
Inc 1 st at each end of next and 2 foll 28th rows. (30 sts)
Work 27 rows, ending with a WS row.
Place markers at both ends of last row – these markers match markers at top of other shaped row-end edges of Sides.
Work 20 rows.
Place markers at both ends of last row – these markers match markers at other ends of cast-on edge of Sides.
Work 68 rows, ending with a WS row.
Cast (bind) off.

FINISHING

Sew in all loose ends, then block and press the pieces.
Insert zipper between cast-off (bound-off) edges of Top Gusset sections.
Join cast-on and cast-off (bound-off) edges of Gusset and Strap to form one large loop. Matching appropriate markers and gusset seam to centre of cast-on edge of Sides, sew Gusset to cast-on and row-end edges of Sides, leaving strap section free. Sew row-end edges of top gussets in place across strap.

PIPING

Using 6.50mm (US 10½) dpns and B, cast on 3 sts.
Row 1: K3, *without turning work slip these 3 sts to opposite end of needle and bring yarn to opposite end of work, pulling it quite tightly across WS of work, now knit these 3 sts again; rep from * until piping fits around entire row-end edge of Gusset and Strap.
Cast (bind) off.
Join ends of Piping, then neatly sew in place as in photograph.
Make and attach a second length of Piping in exactly the same way.
Insert buckram into base of Bag, trimming it to fit as necessary, and carefully sew in place.

DESIGNED BY

Fair Isle Carpet Bag

This bag is the ideal travelling companion; it's good-looking, will hold cabin essentials on a flight and will see you through both daytime meetings and evening parties. What more could a girl want!

YARN

Rowan Big Wool (100% merino wool), approx.
100g (3½ oz)/80m (87yd) per ball
   Two balls of White Hot 001 **(A)**
   One ball of Linen 048 **(B)**
   One ball of Whoosh 014 **(C)**
   One ball of Glamour 036 **(D)**
   One ball of Bohemian 028 **(E)**
   One ball of Wild Berry 025 **(F)**
Coats Anchor Tapisserie Wool (100% wool), approx.
10m (11yd) per skein
   Two skeins of red 8202 **(G)**

NEEDLES

Pair of 15.00mm (US 19) knitting needles
Pair of 4.00mm (US 6) knitting needles

EXTRAS

Stitch holder
Four 38mm (1½ in) diameter self-cover buttons
Piece of lining fabric 50cm by 79cm (19½ in by 31in)
Sewing needle and thread
Six removable stitch markers (or use short lengths of
waste yarn)
Decorative crystal brooch (optional)
Tapestry needle

TENSION (GAUGE)

7 sts and 10½ rows = 10cm (4in) square measured over
St st using 15.00mm (US 19) needles and Rowan Big Wool.

MEASUREMENTS

Completed bag is 39cm (15½ in) wide, 29cm (11½ in) tall
and 16cm (6¼ in) deep.

SKILL LEVEL

Intermediate

SIDES (MAKE 2)

Using 15.00mm (US 19) needles and A, cast on 37 sts.

Row 1 (RS): Knit.

Row 2: Purl.

Starting with a knit row, work 21 rows in St st from chart A, ending with a RS row.

Row 24: With A, purl.

Row 25: With A, knit.

Cast (bind) off.

GUSSET

Using 15.00mm (US 19) needles and B, cast on 12 sts.

Starting with a knit row, work 25 rows in St st, ending with a RS row. (This section fits down first row-end edge of Sides.)

Place markers at both ends of last row – these match to first lower corners of Sides.

Cont in garter st until Gusset, from markers, fits across cast-on edge of Side section, ending with a WS row.

Place markers at both ends of last row – these match to second lower corners of Sides.

Starting with a knit row, work 25 rows in St st, ending with a RS row. (This section fits up other row-end edge of Sides.)

Next row (WS): Knit (to form fold line).

Place markers at both ends of last row – these match to first top corners of Sides.

Work in St st for 5 rows more, ending with a WS row.

SHAPE OPENING

Next row (RS): With C, k6 and turn, leaving rem 6 sts on a holder.

Work in St st with C for 28 rows more, ending with a RS row.

Change to B.

Starting with a purl row, work in St st with B for 5 rows.

Cast (bind) off.

Return to sts left on holder and rejoin C with RS facing.

Starting with a knit row, work in St st with C for 29 rows, ending with a RS row.

Change to B.

Starting with a purl row, work in St st with B for 5 rows.

Cast (bind) off.

HANDLES (MAKE 2)

Using 15.00mm (US 19) needles and A, cast on 21 sts.

Starting with a knit row, work 10 rows in St st from chart B, ending with a WS row.

Cast (bind) off.

BUTTON COVERS (MAKE 4)

Using 4.00mm (US 6) needles and G, cast on 8 sts.

Starting with a knit row, work in St st, kfb at each end of 3rd and foll 2 RS rows. (14 sts)

Work 5 rows, ending with a WS row.

Dec 1 st at each end of next and foll 2 alt rows. (8 sts)

Work 1 row.

Cast (bind) off.

FINISHING

Sew in all loose ends, then block and press the pieces.

From lining fabric, cut out same size pieces as Sides and Gusset, adding seam allowance along all edges.

At cast-off (bound-off) end of Gusset, join central row-end edges for last 5 rows. Join cast-on edge to cast-off (bound-off) edges to form one long loop. Matching markers and gusset seam to corners of Sides, sew Gusset to outer edges of both Sides.

Make up lining fabric in same way as knitted sections. Slip lining inside Bag, turn under raw edges around opening along upper edge and neatly slip stitch in place.

Fold Handles in half and join cast-on edge to cast-off (bound-off) edge to form a tube. Fold Handle flat, with seam running centrally along back of tube, and sew ends closed. Using photograph as a guide, sew Handles to top of Sides, positioning ends of Handles approx. 10cm (4in) apart.

Following manufacturer's instructions, cover buttons with knitted Button Covers. Attach completed buttons to ends of Handles as in photograph.

If desired, attach decorative brooch to one Side between ends of Handles, as in photograph.

Chart A

Chart B

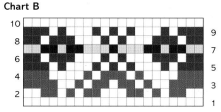

Key

- □ A
- ■ B
- ■ C
- ▦ D
- ▨ E
- ▨ F

UNDER COVER

If you prefer, you can cover the buttons with circles of fabric. Choose a plain colour to complement your yarn choices and cover the buttons according to the instructions that come with your kit.

DESIGNED BY

Tweedy Shopper

A capacious shopping bag that will happily swallow all sorts of goodies, whether you are shopping for salad or shoes. The pretty crochet frill and flower are simple to make, so are perfect for beginners to crochet.

YARN

Debbie Bliss Donegal Chunky Tweed (100% wool), approx. 100g (3½ oz)/100m (109yd) per skein

Two skeins of Peacock 09 **(A)**

GGH Bel Air (90% merino wool, 10% nylon), approx. 50g (1¾ oz)/130m (142yd) per ball

Two balls of Mauve 02 **(B)**

Coats Anchor Tapisserie Wool (100% wool), approx. 10m (11yd) per skein

One skein of lime 9274 **(C)**

NEEDLES

Pair of 9.00mm (US 13) knitting needles

One 6.00mm (J/10) crochet hook

EXTRAS

Four 25mm (1in) diameter red buttons

Stitch holder

Piece of card (for base) 36cm by 8cm (14in by 3in)

Tapestry needle

TENSION (GAUGE)

10 sts and 15 rows = 10cm (4in) square measured over St st using 9.00mm (US 13) needles and A.

MEASUREMENTS

Completed bag is 36cm (14in) wide, 42cm (16½ in) tall and 8cm (3in) deep.

SKILL LEVEL

Beginner

SPECIAL ABBREVIATIONS

See page 255 for information on trtog (dctog).

SIDES AND BASE

Using 9.00mm (US 13) needles and A, cast on 36 sts.

Row 1 (RS): Purl.

Row 2: Knit.

Rep these 2 rows . (forming Rev st st) for 38cm (15in), ending with a WS row.

Place markers at both ends of last row – these denote start of base section.

Next row (RS): Knit.

Next row: Purl.

Rep these 2 rows (forming St st) until work measures 8cm (3in) from markers, ending with a WS row.

Place markers at both ends of last row – these denote end of base section.

Starting with a purl row, work in Rev st st until work measures 38cm (15in) from second set of markers, ending with a WS row.

Cast (bind) off.

GUSSETS (BOTH ALIKE)

Using 9.00mm (US 13) needles and A, with WS facing (so that 'seam' shows on RS) pick up and knit 12 sts along row-end edge of Sides and Base between markers denoting base.

Starting with a purl row, work in Rev st st until Gusset measures 32cm (12½ in) from pick-up row, ending with a WS row.

DIVIDE FOR SIDE OPENINGS

Next row (RS): P6 and turn, leaving rem 6 sts on a holder.

Cont in Rev st st on this set of 6 sts

only until Gusset measures 38cm (15in) from pick-up row, ending with a WS row. Cast (bind) off.

Return to sts left on holder, rejoin A with RS facing and p to end.

Cont in Rev st st on this set of 6 sts only until Gusset measures 38cm (15in) from pick-up row, ending with a WS row. Cast (bind) off.

CROCHET EDGING

Sew row-end edges of Gussets to corresponding row-end edges of Sides, matching cast-off (bound-off) edges of Gussets to cast-on (or cast-off (bound-off)) edges of Sides – sew seams with WS together so that seams show on RS. Using 6.00mm (J/10) crochet hook and B, with RS facing attach yarn at base of one Gusset opening and work one round of dc (sc) evenly around entire upper opening edge, ensuring number of dc (sc) worked is divisible by 4 and ending with ss (sl st) to first dc (sc).

Next round: 1 ch (does NOT count as st), 1 dc (sc) into each dc (sc) to end, ss (sl st) to first dc (sc).

Rep last round once more.

Next round: 1 ch (does NOT count as st), 1 dc (sc) into first dc (sc), *miss 1 dc (sc), 5 tr (dc) into next dc (sc), miss 1 dc (sc), 1 dc (sc) into next dc (sc); rep from * to end, replacing dc (sc) at end of last rep with ss (sl st) to first dc (sc).

Fasten off.

HANDLES (MAKE 2)

Using 9.00mm (US 13) needles and A, cast on 6 sts.

Starting with a knit row, work 37 rows in St st, ending with a RS row.

Cast (bind) off.

FLOWER

Using 6.00mm (J/10) crochet hook and C, make 4 ch and join with ss (sl st) to form a ring.

Round 1: 1 ch (does NOT count as st), 8 dc (sc) into ring, ss (sl st) to first dc (sc) (8 sts).

Round 2: 3 ch, tr3tog (dc3tog) into first dc (sc), *3 ch, 1 dc (sc) into centre ring**, 3 ch, miss next dc (sc) of round 1, tr3tog (dc3tog) into next dc (sc); rep from * to end, ending last rep at **, 1 ss (sl st) into first of 3 ch at beg of round, 6 ch, 1 ss (sl st) into 2nd ch from hook, 1 ss (sl st) into each of next 4 ch (to form stem).

Fasten off.

FINISHING

Sew in all loose ends, then block and press the pieces.

Run gathering threads (with A) across top of Gussets just below opening and pull up to gather top of Gusset to 5cm (2in) wide. Fasten off securely. Using photograph as a guide, sew Handles to top of Sides, positioning ends of Handles approx. 14cm (5½in) apart. Attach buttons to ends of

Handles as in photograph. With A, attach Flower near end of one Handle by working several straight stitches radiating out from centre of Flower. Trim card to fit base of Bag and slip inside Bag and secure in place.

SHOP, DON'T DROP

If you are a keen shopper and like to fill your shopping bag, you can line it to make it stronger. Before sewing the gussets to the sides, lay the bag flat on a piece of heavy cotton fabric and draw around it, adding seam allowance along all edges. Make up the lining in the same way as the bag. After finishing the bag, slip the lining into it. Turn under raw edges around upper edge and neatly slip stitch in place. You can also stitch lengths of grosgrain ribbon to the backs of the handles to stop them stretching.

Knitting Basics

TENSION (GAUGE) AND SELECTING CORRECT NEEDLE SIZE

Tension (gauge) can differ quite dramatically between knitters, because individuals hold the needles and yarn in varying ways, and variations in tension (gauge) will affect the size of the finished project. So if your tension (gauge) does not match that stated in the pattern, to ensure a successful result, you should change your needle size following this simple rule:

- If your knitting is too loose, you will have fewer stitches and rows than the given tension (gauge), and you will need to change to a smaller needle to make the stitch size smaller.
- If your knitting is too tight, you will have more stitches and rows than the given tension (gauge), and you will need to change to a thicker needle to make the stitches bigger.

Please note that if the projects in this book are not knitted to the correct tension (gauge), yarn quantities will be affected.

KNITTING A TENSION (GAUGE) SWATCH

No matter how excited you are about a new knitting project, take time to knit a tension (gauge) swatch for accurate sizing. Using the same needles, yarn and stitch pattern as those that will be used for the main work, knit a sample at least 12.5cm (5in) square. Wash your swatch in the same way as you will the finished project and smooth it out on a flat surface, but do not stretch unless specified in the pattern.

When it is dry, to check the stitch tension (gauge), place a ruler horizontally on the sample, measure 10cm (4in) across and mark with a pin at each end. Count the number of stitches between the pins. To check the row tension (gauge), place a ruler vertically on the sample, measure 10cm (4in) and mark with pins. Count the number of rows between the pins. If the number of stitches and rows is greater than specified in the pattern, make a new swatch using larger needles; if it is less, make a new swatch using smaller needles.

BLOCKING

Wet blocking your knitted pieces makes finishing easier and ensures a neater end result. Gently wash your pieces as recommended on the yarn ball band, lay them on a flat surface and ease into the desired shape and size (as specified in the pattern). If necessary (for example, with lace knitting), use pins to stretch the pieces to size and open the pattern out, then allow to dry.

MAKING A SLIP KNOT

A slip knot is the basis of all cast-on techniques and is therefore the starting point for almost everything you do in knitting and crochet.

1

1 Wind the yarn around two fingers twice as shown. Insert a knitting needle through the first (front) strand and under the second (back) one.

2

2 Using the needle, pull the back strand through the front one to form a loop.

3

3 Holding the loose ends of the yarn with your left hand, pull the needle upwards, thus tightening the knot. Pull the ball end of the yarn again to tighten the knot further.

CASTING ON

'Casting on' is the term used for making a row of stitches to be used as a foundation for your knitting.

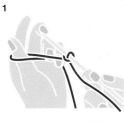

1 Make a slip knot 100cm (40in) from the end of the yarn (or less if casting on only a few stitches). Hold the needle in your right hand with the ball end of the yarn over your index finger. *Wind the loose end of the yarn around your left thumb.

2 Insert the point of the needle under the first strand of yarn on your thumb.

3 With your right index finger, take the ball end of the yarn over the point of the needle.

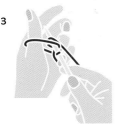

4 Pull a loop through to form the first stitch. Remove your left thumb from the yarn. Pull the loose end to secure the stitch. Repeat from * until the required number of stitches have been cast on.

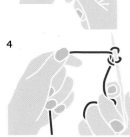

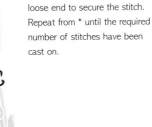

CONTINENTAL CAST ON

This technique produces an edge that has elasticity, so it is a good choice for socks. You need to calculate how much yarn you will use – it is best to allow 2cm (½in) per stitch. Measure out the correct amount of yarn, then make a slip knot.

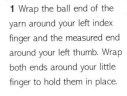

1 Wrap the ball end of the yarn around your left index finger and the measured end around your left thumb. Wrap both ends around your little finger to hold them in place.

2 *Holding the needle in your right hand, put the tip of it up through the loop around your thumb.

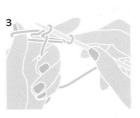

3 Now take it down through the loop around your index finger and then back under the loop on your thumb. Slip your thumb out of its loop, making sure you don't drop the loop off the needle.

4 Using your left thumb, pull the new loop on the needle tight to compete the stitch. Repeat from * until the required number of stitches have been cast on.

LOOP CAST ON

This is a very simple way to cast on. It is useful when a pattern requires you to cast on new stitches at the end of a row.

1

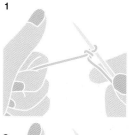

1 Make a slip knot approx. 20cm (8in) from the end of the yarn. Hold the needle in your right hand and use your fingers to keep the loose end of the yarn out of the way. Hold the ball end of the yarn in your left hand.

2

2 *Pass the yarn around your left thumb.

3 Slip the needle tip under the loop around your thumb.

3

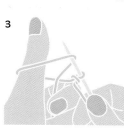

4 Pull your thumb out of the loop and tug on the yarn to tighten up the stitch. Repeat from * until the required number of stitches have been cast on.

4

THE BASIC STITCHES

Knit and purl stitches form the basis of all knitted fabrics. The knit stitch is the easiest to learn and once you have mastered this you can move on to the purl stitch, which is the reverse of the knit stitch.

KNIT STITCH

1

1 Hold the needle with the cast-on stitches in your left hand, with the loose yarn at the back of the work. Insert the right-hand needle from left to right into the front of the first stitch on the left-hand needle.

2

2 Wrap the yarn from left to right over the point of the right-hand needle.

3 Draw the yarn through the stitch, thus forming a new stitch on the right-hand needle.

3

4 Slip the original stitch off the left-hand needle, keeping the new stitch on the right-hand needle.

4

5 To knit a row, repeat steps 1 to 4 until all the stitches have been transferred from the left-hand needle to the right-hand needle. Turn the work, transferring the needle with the stitches to your left hand to work the next row.

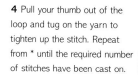

PURL STITCH

1

2

3

4

1 Hold the needle with the stitches in your left hand, with the loose yarn at the front of the work. Insert the right-hand needle from right to left into the front of the first stitch on the left-hand needle.

2 Wrap the yarn from right to left, up and over the point of the right-hand needle.

3 Draw the yarn through the stitch, thus forming a new stitch on the right-hand needle.

4 Slip the original stitch off the left-hand needle, keeping the new stitch on the right-hand needle.

5 To purl a row, repeat steps 1 to 4 until all the stitches have been transferred from the left-hand needle to the right-hand needle. Turn the work, transferring the needle with the stitches to your left hand to work the next row.

INCREASING AND DECREASING

Many projects will require some shaping, whether just to add interest or to make the various sections fit together properly. Shaping is achieved by increasing or decreasing the number of stitches you are working.

INCREASING

The simplest method of increasing one stitch is to work into the front and back of the same stitch.

On a knit row, knit into the front of the stitch to be increased, then before slipping it off the needle, place the right-hand needle behind the left-hand one and knit again into the back of the stitch. Slip the original stitch off the left-hand needle. This is known as kfb. On a purl row, purl into the front of the stitch to be increased, then before slipping it off the needle, purl again into the back of it (pfb). Slip the original stitch off the left-hand needle.

DECREASING

The simplest method of decreasing one stitch is to work two stitches together.

On a knit row, insert the right-hand needle from left to right through two stitches instead of one, then knit them together as one stitch. This is called knit two together (k2tog).

On a purl row, insert the right-hand needle from right to left through two stitches instead of one, then purl them together as one stitch. This is called purl two together (p2tog).

INTARSIA STITCHES

'Intarsia' refers to patterns that are worked in large blocks of colour, requiring a separate ball of yarn for each area of colour.

DIAGONAL COLOUR CHANGE WITH A SLANT TO THE LEFT

DIAGONAL COLOUR CHANGE WITH A SLANT TO THE RIGHT

VERTICAL COLOUR CHANGE

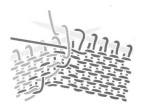

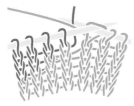

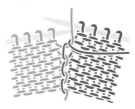

On a wrong-side row, with the yarns at the front of the work, take the first colour over the second colour, drop it, then pick up the second colour underneath the first colour, thus crossing the two strands of yarn over one another.

On a right-side row, with the yarns at the back of the work, take the first colour over the second colour, drop it, then pick up the second colour underneath the first colour, thus crossing the two strands.

Work in the first colour to the colour change, then drop the first colour, pick up the second colour underneath the first colour, thus crossing the two strands of yarn before working the next stitch in the second colour. After a colour change, work the first stitch firmly to prevent a gap forming.

FAIR ISLE STITCHES

In Fair Isle patterns (also called 'stranded knitting'), the colour yarn that is not in use is left at the back of the work until needed. The loops formed by this are called 'floats' and it is important that they are not pulled too tightly when working the next stitch in that colour, as this will pucker your knitting.

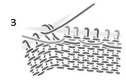
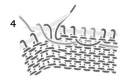

1 On a knit row, hold the first colour in your right hand and the second colour in your left hand. Knit the required number of stitches as usual with the first colour, carrying the second colour loosely across the wrong side of the work.

2 To knit a stitch in the second colour, insert the right-hand needle into the next stitch, then draw a loop through from the yarn held in the left hand, carrying the yarn in the right hand loosely across the wrong side until required.

3 On a purl row, hold the yarns as for the knit rows. Purl the required number of stitches as usual with the first colour, carrying the second colour loosely across these stitches on the wrong side of the work.

4 To purl a stitch in the second colour, insert the right-hand needle into the next stitch, then draw a loop through from the yarn held in the left hand, carrying the yarn in the right hand loosely across the wrong side until required.

- -

CASTING (BINDING) OFF

This is the most common method of securing stitches at the end of a piece of knitting. The cast-off (bound-off) edge should have the same 'give' or elasticity as the fabric; cast (bind) off in the stitch used for the main fabric unless the pattern directs otherwise.

KNITWISE

Knit two stitches. *Using the point of the left-hand needle, lift the first stitch on the right-hand needle over the second, then drop it off the needle. Knit the next stitch and repeat from * until all stitches have been worked off the left-hand needle and only one stitch remains on the right-hand needle. Cut the yarn, leaving enough to sew in the end. Thread the end through the stitch, then slip the stitch off the needle. Draw the yarn up firmly to fasten off.

PURLWISE

Purl two stitches. *Using the point of the left-hand needle, lift the first stitch on the right-hand needle over the second and drop it off the needle. Purl the next stitch and repeat from * until all the stitches have been worked off the left-hand needle and only one stitch remains on the right-hand needle. Cut the yarn, leaving enough to sew in the end. Thread the end through the stitch, then slip the stitch off the needle. Draw the yarn up firmly to fasten off.

Crochet Basics

TENSION (GAUGE)

As in knitting, this refers the number of rows and stitches per centimetre or inch, usually measured over a 10cm (4in) square. The tension (gauge) will determine the size of the finished item. The correct tension (gauge) is given at the beginning of each pattern. Crochet a small swatch, using the recommended yarn and hook, to make sure you are working to the correct tension (gauge). If your work is too loose (too few stitches to 10cm or 4in), choose a hook that is one size smaller; if your work is too tight (too many stitches), choose a hook the next size up. When making clothes, it is important to check tension (gauge) before you start; it is not worth making something the wrong size. When measuring work, lay it on a flat surface and always measure at the centre, rather than at the side edges.

CHAIN STITCH

1

2

3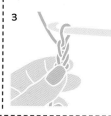

1 Place a slip knot on the hook and hold it in your right hand. Hold the yarn in your left hand, keeping a good tension on the tail end of the yarn. With the yarn sitting to the reverse of the hook, turn the hook so that it is facing away from you.

2 Push the crochet hook against the yarn, then rotate the hook in order to catch the yarn around the hook. Draw the yarn through the loop on the hook.

3 Repeat Step 2 to create more chain stitches. You will need to reposition the tensioning fingers of your left hand every couple of stitches to ensure a good tension on the yarn.

BASIC STITCHES

Start by making a series of chains – around 10 will be enough. Now you're ready to practise the following stitches. In crochet, the same stitches are known by different names in the UK and the US; we have given US terms in brackets throughout.

SLIP STITCH (SS) (SL ST)

1

1 This is the shortest stitch and mostly used for joining and shaping. Insert the hook into a stitch or chain (always remember to insert the hook under both strands of the stitch), take the yarn over the hook from the back to the front, and draw the hook through the stitch and the loop on the hook. You are left with just 1 loop on the hook. This is 1 slip stitch.

DOUBLE CROCHET (DC) (SINGLE CROCHET (SC))

1

2

1 Insert the hook into the second chain from the hook, take the yarn over the hook and draw the loop through.

2 Yarn over and draw the hook through both loops on the hook; 1 loop on the hook. This is 1 double (single) crochet.

3 Repeat into the next stitch or chain until you've reached the end of the row. Make 1 chain stitch – this is your turning chain – then turn the work and work 1 double (single) crochet into each stitch of the previous row, ensuring that you insert the hook under both loops of the stitch you are crocheting into.

HALF TREBLE CROCHET (HTR) (HALF DOUBLE CROCHET (HDC))

1

1 Take yarn over hook before inserting the hook into the third chain from the hook, yarn over, draw 1 loop through the work, yarn over, draw through all 3 loops on the hook; 1 loop on the hook. This is 1 half treble (half double) crochet.

2 When you reach the end of the row, make 2 chains – this counts as the first stitch of the next row. Turn the work, skip the first half treble (half double) crochet of the previous row and insert the hook into the second stitch of the new row. Continue to work until the end of the row. At the end of the row, work the last half treble (half double) crochet into the top of the turning chain of the row below.

TREBLE CROCHET (TR) (DOUBLE CROCHET (DC))

1

2

1 Start by wrapping the yarn over the hook and insert the hook into the fourth chain from the hook, yarn over, draw 1 loop through the work.

2 Yarn over, draw through the first 2 loops on the hook, yarn over, draw through the remaining 2 loops on the hook; 1 loop on the hook. This is 1 treble (double) crochet.

3 When you reach the end of the row, make 3 chains. These count as the first stitch of the next row. Turn the work and skip the first treble (double) crochet of the previous row; insert the hook into the second stitch of the new row. Continue to work until the end of the row, inserting the last treble (double) crochet into the top of the turning chain of the row below.

BASIC TECHNIQUES

As well as working from right to left in rows, crochet can also be worked in a circular fashion (referred to as working in the round), or even in a continuous spiral to make seamless items such as hats, bags and other rounded objects.

MAKING FABRIC – WORKING IN ROWS

1

2

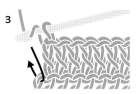

3

1 Make as many chain stitches as you require. This row is called the base chain. Insert the hook into the second chain from the hook (not counting the chain on the hook) for double (single) crochet, or the third chain from the hook for treble (double) crochet.

2 Work from right to left, inserting the hook under two of the three threads in each chain.

3 When you reach the end of the row, work one or more turning chains, depending on the height of the stitch.

Turning chains should be worked as follows:
Double (single) crochet: 1 chain.
Half treble (half double) crochet: 2 chains.
Treble (double) crochet: 3 chains.
Double treble (treble): 4 chains.
Triple treble (double treble): 5 chains.

Now turn the work to begin working on the next row (remember always to turn your work in the same direction). When working in double (single) crochet, insert the hook into the first stitch in the new row and work each stitch to the end of the row, excluding the turning chain. For all other stitches, unless the pattern states otherwise, the turning chain counts as the first stitch. Skip 1 stitch and work each stitch to the end of the row, including the top of the turning chain.

MAKING FABRIC – WORKING IN THE ROUND

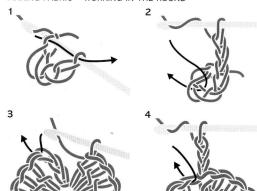

1

2

3

4

1 Start by making a series of chains, then join the last chain to the first with a slip stitch to form a ring.

2 To make the first round, work a starting chain to the height of the stitch you are working in. Then work as many stitches as you need into the centre of the ring.

3 Finish the round with a slip stitch into the first stitch.

4 Begin the second and subsequent rounds with a starting chain (worked the same way as a turning chain, with the number of chains depending on the stitch you are working: see page 250). Then insert the hook under the top 2 loops of each stitch in the previous round. At the end of the round, join to the top of the starting chain with a slip stitch, as in step 2.

INCREASING

As with knitting, fabric is often shaped by increasing the number of stitches in a row or round. To increase, simply work an additional stitch into the next stitch. A single increase is made by working 2 stitches into the same stitch. You can of course increase by more than 1 stitch at a time.

DECREASING

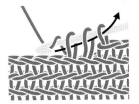

DC2TOG (SC2TOG)

To decrease 1 stitch in double (single) crochet, insert hook into next stitch, yarn over, draw through the work, insert hook into the next stitch, yarn over, draw through the work, yarn over, draw through all 3 loops, leaving just 1 loop on the hook.

DC3TOG (SC3TOG)

To decrease by 2 stitches in double (single) crochet, work 3 stitches together, by working as for dc2tog (sc2tog) until you have 3 loops on the hook. Insert the hook into the next stitch, yarn over, draw through the work, yarn over and draw through all 4 loops.

TR2TOG (DC2TOG)

To decrease 1 stitch in treble (double) crochet, yarn over, insert hook into next stitch, yarn over, draw through work, yarn over, draw through 2 loops, yarn over, insert hook into next stitch, yarn over, draw through work, yarn over, draw through 2 loops, yarn over, draw through all 3 loops.

FINISHING

There are various ways of sewing up seams.

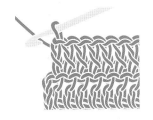

FASTENING OFF

Cut the yarn, leaving roughly 13cm (5in). Make 1 chain and draw the tail through the chain and pull firmly. Weave the end a few centimetres or an inch in one direction and then back the other way for a neat and secure finish.

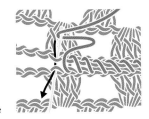

FLAT STITCH

This seam creates an almost invisible join. Lay the two sections right-side up, with the stitches aligned. Using a tapestry needle, insert under the lower half of the edge stitch on one section, then under the upper half of the edge stitch on the opposite section.

Abbreviations and Special Techniques

KNITTING

alt = alternate/alternating

B1 = bring yarn to front (RS) of work, slip a bead up close to stitch just worked, slip next stitch purlwise, then take yarn to back (WS) of work, leaving bead sitting in front of slipped stitch.

BC = Back cross: slip 1 st onto cn and hold at back, k2, then p1 from cn.

beg = beginning

BS = Bead stitch

C2F = Slip 1 st onto cn and hold at back of work, k1, then k1 from cn.

C4L = Slip next 2 sts onto cn and hold in front of work, k2, then k2 from cn.

C4R = Slip 2 sts onto cn, and hold at back of work, k2, then k2 from cn.

cn = cable needle

CO = cast on

cont = continue/continuing

CP = Bobbly cable pattern

Cr st = Crossed stitch

de = Double eyelet: k2tog, yo, k1, yo, ssk

dec = decrease/decreasing

dpn(s) = double-pointed needle(s)

FC = Front cross: sl 2 sts to cn and hold in front, p1, then k2 from cn.

foll = follow(s)/following

inc = increase/increasing

k = knit

k2tog = knit two sts together

kfb = knit into front and back of stitch

LH = left-hand

lk2tog = Lifted k2tog: slip next st, lift bar between next 2 sts and place on LH needle with regular mount (leading edge is in front of needle), return slipped st to LH needle with reverse mount (leading edge of st is behind needle), k2tog tbl.

lp2tog = Lifted p2tog: slip next st purlwise, lift bar between next 2 sts and place on LH needle with reverse mount, return slipped st to LH needle with regular mount, p2tog.

M = marker

m1 = make one st: lift the horizontal strand between the st just worked and next st, then knit through back of this thread.

m1l = Make 1 stitch slanting to the left: insert the left needle from front to back into the bar between the needles. With the right needle, knit through the back.

m1r = Make 1 stitch slanting to the right: insert the left needle from back to front into the bar between the needles. With the right needle, knit through the front.

MB = Make bobble: [k1, yo, k1, yo, k1] into 1 st, turn, p5, turn, k5, turn, p2tog, k1, p2tog tbl, turn, k3tog.

MC = main colour

MK = Make knot: [k1, p1, k1, p1, k1, p1, k1] into 1 st, making 7 sts from one; then with point of LH needle pass the second, third, fourth, fifth, sixth and seventh stitches on the RH needle separately over the last st made, completing the knot.

N = needle

p = purl

p2tog = purl two sts together

patt = pattern

pfb = purl into front and back of stitch

PK = Purl knot: insert RH needle under strand running between first and second sts on LH needle and loosely draw loop through, insert RH needle above same strand between sts and loosely draw through a second loop, bring yarn to front (RS) of work, p1, lift the 2 loops over this p st and off RH needle.

PM = place/placing marker

prev = previous

psso = pass slipped stitch over

rem = remain(s)/remaining

rep = repeat

Rev St st = reverse stocking (stockinette) stitch

RH = right-hand

rnd = round

RS = right side

sep = separate

skpo = slip 1 st knitwise, knit 1 st, pass slipped stitch over

sl = slip/slipped

sl1p = slip 1 st purlwise

SM = slip marker

sppo = slip 1 st purlwise, purl 1 st, pass slipped stitch over